Manhattan Review ®

Test Prep & Admissions Consulting

Turbocharge Your GRE:
Text Completion & Sentence Equivalence Guide

part of the 3rd Edition Series

April 20th, 2016

D1591638

- ☐ *Intuitive explanations of all concepts relevant for the GRE takers*

- ☐ *Detailed process of "Pre-empting blanks with a proven strategy"*

- ☐ *Complete & Challenging Training Sets:*

    - *100 Sentence Equivalence questions*
    - *100 Text Completion questions*

- ☐ *Ample number of questions with at least one tricky option*

- ☐ *Comprehensive explanations*

- ☐ *Contextually relevant meaning of each option word*

www.manhattanreview.com

Copyright and Terms of Use

Copyright and Trademark

All materials herein (including names, terms, trademarks, designs, images, and graphics) are the property of Manhattan Review, except where otherwise noted. Except as permitted herein, no such material may be copied, reproduced, displayed or transmitted or otherwise used without the prior written permission of Manhattan Review. You are permitted to use material herein for your personal, noncommercial use, provided that you do not combine such material into a combination, collection, or compilation of material. If you have any questions regarding the use of the material, please contact Manhattan Review at info@manhattanreview.com.

This material may make reference to countries and persons. The use of such references is for hypothetical and demonstrative purposes only.

Terms of Use

By using this material, you acknowledge and agree to the terms of use contained herein.

No Warranties

This material is provided without warranty, either express or implied, including the implied warranties of merchantability, of fitness for a particular purpose and noninfringement. Manhattan Review does not warrant or make any representations regarding the use, accuracy or results of the use of this material. This material may make reference to other source materials. Manhattan Review is not responsible in any respect for the content of such other source materials, and disclaims all warranties and liabilities with respect to the other source materials.

Limitation on Liability

Manhattan Review shall not be responsible under any circumstances for any direct, indirect, special, punitive, or consequential damages ("Damages") that may arise from the use of this material. In addition, Manhattan Review does not guarantee the accuracy or completeness of its course materials, which are provided "as is" with no warranty, express or implied. Manhattan Review assumes no liability for any Damages from errors or omissions in the material, whether arising in contract, tort or otherwise.

GRE is a registered trademark of the Educational Testing Services.
ETS does not endorse, nor is it affiliated in any way with, the owner of this product or any content herein.

10-Digit International Standard Book Number: (ISBN: 1-62926-083-5)
13-Digit International Standard Book Number: (ISBN: 978-1-62926-083-9)

Last updated on April 20th, 2016.

Manhattan Review, 275 Madison Avenue, Suite 1429, New York, NY 10016.
Phone: +1 (212) 316-2000. E-Mail: info@manhattanreview.com. Web: www.manhattanreview.com

About the Turbocharge your GRE Series

The Turbocharge Your GRE Series consists of 13 guides that cover everything you need to know for a great score on the GRE. Widely respected among GRE educators worldwide, Manhattan Review's GRE prep books offer the most professional GRE instruction available anywhere. Now in its updated 3rd edition, the full series is carefully designed to provide GRE test-takers with exhaustive GRE preparation for optimal test scores. Manhattan Review's GRE prep books teach you how to prepare for each of the different GRE testing areas with a thorough instructional methodology that is rigorous yet accessible and enjoyable. You'll learn everything necessary about each test section in order to receive your best possible GRE scores. The full series covers GRE verbal, quantitative, and writing concepts from the most basic through the most advanced levels, and is therefore a great study resource for all stages of GRE preparation. Students who work through all books in the series significantly improve their knowledge of GRE subject matter and learn the most strategic approaches to taking and vanquishing the GRE.

- ☐ **GRE Math Essentials Guide** (ISBN: 978-1-62926-073-0)
- ☐ **GRE Number Properties Guide** (ISBN: 978-1-62926-074-7)
- ☐ **GRE Arithmetic Guide** (ISBN: 978-1-62926-075-4
- ☐ **GRE Algebra Guide** (ISBN: 978-1-62926-076-1
- ☐ **GRE Geometry Guide** (ISBN: 978-1-62926-077-8)
- ☐ **GRE Word Problems Guide** (ISBN: 978-1-62926-078-5)
- ☐ **GRE Combinatorics & Probability Guide** (ISBN: 978-1-62926-079-2)
- ☐ **GRE Sets, Statistics & Data Interpretation Guide** (ISBN: 978-1-62926-080-8)
- ☐ **GRE Quantitative Question Bank** (ISBN: 978-1-62926-081-5)
- ☐ **GRE Reading Comprehension Guide** (ISBN: 978-1-62926-082-2)
- ■ **GRE Text Completion & Sentence Equivalence Guide** (ISBN: 978-1-62926-083-9)
- ☐ **GRE Analytical Writing Guide** (ISBN: 978-1-62926-084-6)
- ☐ **GRE Vocabulary Builder** (ISBN: 978-1-62926-085-3)

About the Company

Manhattan Review's origin can be traced directly back to an Ivy League MBA classroom in 1999. While teaching advanced quantitative subjects to MBAs at Columbia Business School in New York City, Professor Dr. Joern Meissner developed a reputation for explaining complicated concepts in an understandable way. Prof. Meissner's students challenged him to assist their friends, who were frustrated with conventional test preparation options. In response, Prof. Meissner created original lectures that focused on presenting standardized test content in a simplified and intelligible manner, a method vastly different from the voluminous memorization and so-called tricks commonly offered by others. The new methodology immediately proved highly popular with students, inspiring the birth of Manhattan Review.

Since its founding, Manhattan Review has grown into a multi-national educational services firm, focusing on preparation for the major undergraduate and graduate admissions tests, college admissions consulting, and application advisory services, with thousands of highly satisfied students all over the world. Our GRE material is continuously expanded and updated by the Manhattan Review team, an enthusiastic group of master GRE professionals and senior academics. Our team ensures that Manhattan Review offers the most time-efficient and cost-effective preparation available for the GRE. Please visit www.ManhattanReview.com for further details.

About the Founder

Professor Dr. Joern Meissner has more than 25 years of teaching experience at the graduate and undergraduate levels. He is the founder of Manhattan Review, a worldwide leader in test prep services, and he created the original lectures for its first test preparation classes. Prof. Meissner is a graduate of Columbia Business School in New York City, where he received a PhD in Management Science. He has since served on the faculties of prestigious business schools in the United Kingdom and Germany. He is a recognized authority in the areas of supply chain management, logistics, and pricing strategy. Prof. Meissner thoroughly enjoys his research, but he believes that grasping an idea is only half of the fun. Conveying knowledge to others is even more fulfilling. This philosophy was crucial to the establishment of Manhattan Review, and remains its most cherished principle.

The Advantages of Using Manhattan Review

▶ **Time efficiency and cost effectiveness.**

  – For most people, the most limiting factor of test preparation is time.

  – It takes significantly more teaching experience to prepare a student in less time.

  – Our test preparation approach is tailored for busy professionals. We will teach you what you need to know in the least amount of time.

▶ **Our high-quality and dedicated instructors are committed to helping every student reach her/his goals.**

International Phone Numbers and Official Manhattan Review Websites

Manhattan Headquarters	+1-212-316-2000	www.manhattanreview.com
USA & Canada	+1-800-246-4600	www.manhattanreview.com
Argentina	+1-212-316-2000	www.review.com.ar
Australia	+61-3-9001-6618	www.manhattanreview.com
Austria	+43-720-115-549	www.review.at
Belgium	+32-2-808-5163	www.manhattanreview.be
Brazil	+1-212-316-2000	www.manhattanreview.com.br
Chile	+1-212-316-2000	www.manhattanreview.cl
China	+86-20-2910-1913	www.manhattanreview.cn
Czech Republic	+1-212-316-2000	www.review.cz
France	+33-1-8488-4204	www.review.fr
Germany	+49-89-3803-8856	www.review.de
Greece	+1-212-316-2000	www.review.com.gr
Hong Kong	+852-5808-2704	www.review.hk
Hungary	+1-212-316-2000	www.review.co.hu
India	+1-212-316-2000	www.review.in
Indonesia	+1-212-316-2000	www.manhattanreview.id
Ireland	+1-212-316-2000	www.gmat.ie
Italy	+39-06-9338-7617	www.manhattanreview.it
Japan	+81-3-4589-5125	www.manhattanreview.jp
Malaysia	+1-212-316-2000	www.review.my
Mexico	+1-212-316-2000	www.manhattanreview.mx
Netherlands	+31-20-808-4399	www.manhattanreview.nl
New Zealand	+1-212-316-2000	www.review.co.nz
Philippines	+1-212-316-2000	www.review.ph
Poland	+1-212-316-2000	www.review.pl
Portugal	+1-212-316-2000	www.review.pt
Qatar	+1-212-316-2000	www.review.qa
Russia	+1-212-316-2000	www.manhattanreview.ru
Singapore	+65-3158-2571	www.gmat.sg
South Africa	+1-212-316-2000	www.manhattanreview.co.za
South Korea	+1-212-316-2000	www.manhattanreview.kr
Sweden	+1-212-316-2000	www.gmat.se
Spain	+34-911-876-504	www.review.es
Switzerland	+41-435-080-991	www.review.ch
Taiwan	+1-212-316-2000	www.gmat.tw
Thailand	+66-6-0003-5529	www.manhattanreview.com
Turkey	+1-212-316-2000	www.review.com.tr
United Arab Emirates	+1-212-316-2000	www.manhattanreview.ae
United Kingdom	+44-20-7060-9800	www.manhattanreview.co.uk
Rest of World	+1-212-316-2000	www.manhattanreview.com

Contents

Chapter 1

Welcome

Dear Students,

At Manhattan Review, we constantly strive to provide the best educational content for preparation of standardized tests, putting arduous efforts to make things better and better. This continuous evolution is very important for an examination like the GRE, which too evolves constantly. Sadly, a GRE aspirant is confused with too many options in the market. The challenge is how to choose a book or a tutor that prepares you to reach your goal. Without saying that we are the best, we leave it for you to judge.

This book differs in many aspects from standard books available in the market. Unlike a book from any other prep company, this book discusses the process of solving Sentence Equivalence and Text Completion questions in detail. Each question is explained with a detailed explanation: why the correct answer is right and why the incorrect ones are wrong.

The book boasts of 200 GRE-like quality questions: 100 SE & 100 TC. The approach of "Preempting the blank" is followed in all the questions, this way student can think of a probable answer before hand without getting muddled by cleverly crafted options. Contextually relevant meanings of the option words are provided for all the options; this way the book also acts as a supplement to Vocabulary Builder.

In a nut shell, Manhattan Review's GRE-TC & SE book is holistic and comprehensive in all respects; it is created so because we listen to what students need. Should you have any query, please feel free to write to us at info@manhattanreview.com.

Happy Learning!

Prof. Dr. Joern Meissner
& The Manhattan Review Team

Chapter 2

Concepts of Sentence Equivalence

Sentence Equivalence questions consist of a single sentence with a blank; the blank can be filled with a word or a phrase, making a meaningful sentence. These are very similar to single-blank Text Completion questions but have six options with exactly two correct options.

Let us see the example:

In the Amazon forest, the solid ground shades into a patch of quicksand so _____ that only after you have got down quite a bit into the quicks and will you realize that you are in it.

- ☐ subtly

- ☐ haphazardly

- ☐ perilously

- ☐ vividly

- ☐ randomly

- ☐ surreptitiously

You must select both the correct options to get the credit for the question; there is no partial credit. In the question above, the correct options are 'subtly' and 'surreptitiously'; marking one of 'subtly', 'surreptitiously', and any one of the remaining four options would be treated as an incorrect response.

In the GRE examination, options are not marked with A, B, C, D, E, & F, but with square checkboxes. Though the GRE uses circular radio buttons for questions with one correct answer, for Sentence Equivalence (SE) questions, it uses square checkboxes; this should be your reminder that this question types requires you to select two answer options.

Since it is cumbersome to refer to options without their short references–A, B, C, D, E, & F, we will list options through alphabetized list.

What do Sentence Equivalence questions test?

Let us see what the test-maker, ETS says about this.

According to ETS:

Like Text Completion questions, Sentence Equivalence questions test the ability to reach a conclusion about how a passage should be completed on the basis of partial information but to a greater extent they focus the meaning of the completed whole. Sentence Equivalence questions consist of a single sentence with just one blank, and they ask you to find two choices that both lead to a complete coherent sentence and that produce sentences that mean the same thing.

In a nut-shell, SE questions ask you to...

- Understand the meaning of the sentence from the partial information.

- Understand the logical structure of the sentence.

- Understand hint or clue words or phrases.

- Understand the role of transition or signal word(s), such as, moreover, though, but, etc.

- Understand the contextual meanings of option words.

Let us take the example and develop the approach to solve SE questions.

In the Amazon forest, the solid ground shades into a patch of quicksand so _____ that only after you have got down quite a bit into the quicksand will you realize that you are in it.

  (A) subtly

  (B) haphazardly

  (C) perilously

  (D) vividly

  (E) randomly

  (F) surreptitiously

Let us understand the meaning of the sentence from the partial information.

The sentence states that in the Amazon forest, the solid ground turns into a patch of quicksand in **some way** (**blank**). We have so far no hint about what 'some way' is. The later part of sentence provides us the **hint** for the **fill-in (blank)**. **Some way** is a characteristic that describes that only after getting down quite a bit into the quicksand that one realizes that he/she is in the quicksand. Thus, the change from solid ground into quicksand is not apparent to the walker immediately.

We can deduce that the **fill-in** must be an adjective that describes the process of solid ground turning into quicksand and we must look for options that are adjectives; however in SE questions, all the options would be of the same parts of speech, here, adjectives.

Let us pre-empt the **fill-in**; since the process of change from solid ground into quicksand is not apparent to the walker immediately, we can deduce that it takes place unnoticeably, so the **fill-in** must be contextually relatable words from the near-synonym family of **unnoticeably**.

Do pre-empt the **fill-in** before looking at the options. The anticipated **fill-in** coming out of the understanding of the sentence would act as a reference to look for among options.

Let us understand the meanings of the option words.

(A) subtly – difficult to perceive or understand; mysterious

(B) haphazardly – at random; not in order

(C) perilously – full of risk; hazardously; dangerously

(D) vividly – distinctly, or clearly perceptible; lively; animatedly

(E) randomly – at random; not in order

(F) surreptitiously – done or acted in a stealthy or secret manner

The correct answers would be 'subtly' and 'surreptitiously'. Though 'subtly' and 'surreptitiously' do not strictly mean 'unnoticeably', they are near-synonym pairs to 'unnoticeably'. You would not find an SE question that has a correct answer pair which has unrelated words. The provided sentence will always have a hint and you would not be asked to predict the answer in vacuum.

Options 'haphazardly', 'randomly' and 'perilously' do not explain why the walker wouldn't realize he/she has walked into quicksand. You may encounter an option word or words whose meaning is not known to you; however you may still get through and get the correct answer provided that it seldom occurs with you and you are lucky too. For example, say, you do not know the meaning of the word 'perilously', but as per the analysis of the sentence, we deduced that 'subtly' and 'surreptitiously' are the perfect matches for the blank, and there cannot be three correct options. The downside is that you are not lucky quite often, so the take-away message is: Do learn vocabulary and the contextual meaning of words!

Option 'vividly' would contradict what is stated in the sentence. If the change is so vivid or noticeable, then the walker should realize that he/she has walked into quicksand.

The correct answers are 'subtly' and 'surreptitiously'.

Let us take another example.

Although the play does use some excellent innovative techniques, on the whole, it can hardly be considered _____.

(A) transcendental

(B) outmoded

(C) bequeathed

(D) peculiar

(E) radical

> **(F)** antediluvian

Let us understand the meaning of the sentence from the partial information.

The sentence states that the play uses some innovative techniques in its portrayal; it can hardly be considered **something**. With the use of a transition or **signal** word 'although', we can get the direction of the thought; it means that the following thought would be opposite of what is stated in the first part of the sentence. But with the use of another **hint** phrase **'can hardly be'**, the thought changes the direction again, thus, we can infer that the intention is to establish that the play, on the whole, can hardly be considered **innovative**.

So, we got our pre-empt **fill-in**; it should be contextually relatable words from the near-synonym family of **innovative**.

Let us understand the meanings of the option words.

  (A) transcendental – surpassing all others; superior

  (B) outmoded – out-of-date; old-fashioned; obsolete

  (C) bequeathed – disposed of; passed on; donated

  (D) peculiar – unfamiliar; strange

  (E) radical – sweeping ; fundamental

  (F) antediluvian – ancient; out-of-date; old-fashioned

The correct answers would be 'transcendental' and 'radical'. Though 'transcendental' and 'radical' do not mean 'innovative', they are contextually relatable extended near-synonym pairs to 'innovative'.

This question is a good example to understand that you MUST NOT only look for synonyms of the pre-empt word. You would notice that even the correct option pair–'transcendental' and 'radical' are not synonymous, yet both the words qualify to produce sentences that mean the same thing.

So can there be many words that are not synonymous, yet they make way for the fill-in? Yes, they can! Words, such as, majestic, pioneering, and dazzling can also qualify; however you will not be presented these many options together in the question. Since the sentence "*Although the play does use some excellent innovative techniques, on the whole, it can hardly be considered _____.*" is relatively short thus keeping in mind the wide scope of the fill-in, test-maker would draft options judiciously.

Option words 'outmoded', and 'antediluvian' would convey the opposite meaning of what we want, thus incorrect.

Option 'peculiar' is cleverly drafted option which means unusual, strange, and weird. Though in the absence of 'transcendental' and 'radical', 'unusual (for peculiar)' can qualify from the boundary line; it does not promise a positive undertone for the fill-in. The **fill-in** demands a word that has a positive undertone. Understanding the contextual meaning of 'peculiar' as unusual, strange, and weird, we can surely discard it as a probable option.

Option 'bequeathed' is not relevant. You may find one or two options that are not relevant to the sentence, thus easy to be discarded for the consideration.

The correct answers are 'transcendental' and 'radical'.

Two negatives make positive

There may be a sentence that uses NOT twice, and if the sentence uses contrasting transition or signal word too, the **fill-in** becomes little difficult to pre-empt–whether the **fill-in** would be contextually relatable near-synonym word describing a characteristic.
Let us see an example.

Although Alfred is not deemed iconoclast by the court of law, major section of the society has not absolved him of the charges of _____.

  (A) blasphemy

  (B) conformism

  (C) tolerance

  (D) consecration

  (E) desecration

  (F) lampooning

Let us understand the meaning of the sentence from the partial information.

The meaning of '*Alfred is not deemed iconoclast by the court of law*' simply is that '*Alfred is not rebellion (iconoclast)*' or '**Alfred is a free-thinker or a conformist (antonym of iconoclast)**'. With the usage of signal word '**Although**', we can pre-empt that the following thought would be in contrast to '**Alfred is a conformist**' or it would be '**Alfred is still an iconoclast**'; however with the usage of '**not absolved (pardoned)**' in the second clause '*major section of the society has **not** absolved him of the charges of _____.*', we infer that the society still considers him an iconoclast.

So we got the **fill-in**; it would be contextually relatable near-synonym words from the family of **iconoclasm**.

Let us understand the meanings of the option words.

(A) blasphemy – profanity; irreverence; sacrilege

(B) conformism – conformity; orthodoxy; traditionalism

(C) trepidation – nervousness; apprehension

(D) consecration – sanctification; revering; dedication

(E) desecration – sacrilege; defilement

(F) lampooning – parodying; satirizing

The correct answers would be 'blasphemy' and 'desecration'. Pair of wrong options which are antonyms of iconoclasm–conformism & consecration–are cleverly planted to misguide you.

Options 'trepidation' and 'lampooning' are irrelevant pair of options.

The correct answers are 'blasphemy' and 'desecration'.

Signal or transition words

The following table of signal or transition words, phrases, and structures may help you understand the tone, style, and the meaning of the sentence.

Continuation of thought	Opposing thought	Conclusion
Moreover	However	Therefore
Furthermore	But	Hence
In addition	Despite	So
Similarly	In spite of	Implies
Also	On the contrary	As a result
Too	Nevertheless	Thus
Since	Conversely	In short
Because	Instead	Inferred
Illustrated by	Yet	Consequently
And	Rather than	
: (colon)	Still	
; (semi-colon)	Surprisingly	
	While	
	Although	
	Though	
	Even if	

Process of solving SE questions

(1) Understand the meaning of the sentence from the partial information

(2) Understand the role of transition/signal word(s)

Whether the transition/signal word carries the thought in the same direction or in the opposite direction

(3) Relate hint word(s) or phrase with signal word to pre-empt the fill-in.

(4) Pre-empt the fill-in word(s) or phrase

 (a) Understand the tone of the sentence

  Test-maker may cleverly craft a sarcastic sentence that may seemingly ask for a fill-in word which has a positive undertone, however the correct fill-in word should have a negative undertone and vice-versa

 (b) Be sure to have contextually relatable near-synonym words for pre-empt word(s) or phrase

(5) Understand the meanings of the option words

 (a) Keeping in mind contextually in the mind, select two option words that are best suited for the pre-empt word(s) or phrase

 (b) If you do not know the meaning of all the option words, you may apply process of elimination. If you are able to identify antonyms of fill-in and unrelated words, then other two words are the correct answer. Though it seems simple, it is not easy. The key is to learn vocabulary!

 (c) If among option words you happen to figure out three near-synonym words, eliminated them as they cannot be the correct answers because only two options can be correct in SE questions; however you will seldom find an SE question that has above scenario. Test-makers are clever and they know this trick well.

We have a separate book for vocabulary building.

In the next chapter, you will find 100 Sentence correction questions for practice.

Chapter 3

Sentence Equivalence Questions

1. Avalanche from the Nepal's worst earthquake in its history had almost shattered the neighboring areas of the capital; however NDRF team worked relentlessly day and night to _____ the looming devastation in the capital.

   (A) alleviate

   (B) resuscitate

   (C) mollify

   (D) aggravate

   (E) forestall

   (F) amputate

2. Proud and aggressive, Nash couldn't handle success and remain grounded: the more his dexterity as a mathematical genius increased, the more _____ his personal life became.

   (A) tempestuous

   (B) capricious

   (C) auspicious

   (D) spiritual

   (E) unruffled

   (F) rustic

3. Although it is the most isolated body of water on the planet, Southern Ocean is not exempt from _____, as winds and ocean currents are common and debris is on its waters and shores.

   (A) defilement

   (B) purification

   (C) composure

   (D) imperturbability

   (E) adumbration

   (F) contamination

4. Conditions in the indoor environment that are especially _____ to the growth of fungi are high relative humidity and warmth.

   (A) apposite

   (B) deleterious

   (C) pernicious

   (D) hostile

   (E) inimical

   (F) conducive

5. According to the Vienna convention on the law of treaties, if one party _____ a bilateral treaty, the other party too can terminate the treaty or suspend its operation in whole or in part.

    (A) breaches

    (B) vituperates

    (C) honors

    (D) vitiates

    (E) abrogates

    (F) denigrates

6. He was gruff and _____ but she had always sensed that there was a reason for that, something in his past that had wounded him and kept him from getting too close to anyone else.

    (A) standoffish

    (B) sedulous

    (C) aloof

    (D) partisan

    (E) nubile

    (F) erudite

7. A few nights passed. Josh kept dreaming as usual but what was not usual was that his dreams were illogical and _____. Many of his dreams consisted of him floating lazily in the sky and one dream even depicted him as a cheeseburger being eaten by Robert.

    (A) insightful

    (B) mysterious

    (C) inscrutable

    (D) acerbic

    (E) laconic

    (F) vivid

8. I, the story teller have the benefit of hindsight, while the "I" in this book is still wet behind the ears—a mere _____.

    (A) novice

    (B) dilettante

    (C) tyro

    (D) professional

    (E) aesthete

    (F) anchorite

9. Jainism is one of the world's most ancient religions, and Jain monks lead a life of extreme austerity and _____.

    (A) renunciation

    (B) prodigality

    (C) consternation

    (D) abnegation

    (E) profligacy

    (F) perturbation

10. There are more job openings available in America today than at any other point in history, yet the percentage of adult Americans working or actively looking for a job stands at a very low level: this _____ has bedeviled economists and policymakers alike and is providing fresh fodder for politicians on both sides of the political aisle.

    (A) lampoon

    (B) providence

    (C) conundrum

    (D) quandary

    (E) serendipity

    (F) parody

11. His personality is such that no matter his work contains banal ideas, his followers would still characterize his work as _____.

    (A) orthodox

    (B) bizarre

    (C) original

    (D) paltry

    (E) conventional

    (F) innovative

12. To trap a Fox, first a hole is dug at a forty five degree angle, a shallow depression is scooped out in front of the hole then the trap is covered _____ with finely sifted dirt so that the fox walks over without knowing about the hole until it falls for trap.

    (A) permanently

    (B) imperceptibly

    (C) sporadically

    (D) precariously

    (E) slightly

    (F) unsteadily

13. The project was completed _____ but unintelligently: although every team member worked closely together, the team did not optimize the limited resources.

   (A) competitively

   (B) passionately

   (C) cooperatively

   (D) deviously

   (E) craftily

   (F) amicably

14. Although the students were _____ during the science presentation, the presenter did her best to involve them in active conversation.

   (A) loquacious

   (B) taciturn

   (C) arbitrary

   (D) reticent

   (E) tractable

   (F) garrulous

15. In his memoir, Jeremy Campbell presents himself as having achieved a holistic congruity by having _____ contradictory elements of his life.

   (A) plagiarized

   (B) ostracized

   (C) reconciled

   (D) confined

   (E) resolved

   (F) vilified

16. Overall, the journal presents an unsystematic, superficial view of innovation that you would expect from an amateur _____, not the world's greatest publisher, said the technology expert.

   (A) luddite

   (B) dilettante

   (C) virtuoso

   (D) eremite

   (E) sciolist

   (F) prodigy

17. Lady Gaga, whose artistic works were often flamboyant, was in her private life a surprisingly _____ person: she lived in rented rooms, ate little, and wore drab clothes.

   (A) unostentatious

   (B) audacious

   (C) simple

   (D) unorthodox

   (E) imprudent

   (F) controversial

18. The new short-film by Jacques Carlton is not _____; it is more likely to appeal to an international audience who like short-films with strictly regional themes.

   (A) complex

   (B) domestic

   (C) populist

   (D) provincial

   (E) democratic

   (F) byzantine

19. In his first campaign, senator Rumsfeld ran as an outsider, _____ against a city bureaucracy that he repeatedly described as "bumbling and bungling."

   (A) railing

   (B) corroborating

   (C) edifying

   (D) inveighing

   (E) indoctrinating

   (F) endorsing

20. The understanding that life complexity originated with a microorganism adapting to specific needs is so simple to state and to grasp that there is a tendency to _____ its significance.

   (A) approbate

   (B) articulate

   (C) trivialize

   (D) enunciate

   (E) praise

   (F) underrate

21. Often jettisoning the names their parents gave them, people who enter Hollywood regularly swap the _____ names they were born with for more exotic ones.

    (A) scintillating

    (B) ambiguous

    (C) pedestrian

    (D) evocative

    (E) quotidian

    (F) dubious

22. He cannot be accused of _____ his affection towards his daughter; his behavior towards her betrays his immense love for her.

    (A) lavishing

    (B) stinting

    (C) limiting

    (D) indulging

    (E) propagandizing

    (F) touting

23. The revelation that one of the contestants was a friend left the judge open to charges of lack of _____, yet he remained insistent his assertion that association did not necessarily imply bias.

    (A) composure

    (B) disinterestedness

    (C) disparateness

    (D) impassiveness

    (E) dispassionateness

    (F) clairvoyance

24. Although David feigned great enthusiasm for his employee's project, in reality his interest in it was so _____ as to be almost non-existent.

    (A) perfunctory

    (B) profound

    (C) superficial

    (D) preemptive

    (E) imperative

    (F) ardent

25. His thriftiness should not be confused with _____: he has always been willing to assist those who are in need.

   (A) penuriousness

   (B) parsimoniousness

   (C) indigence

   (D) exuberance

   (E) niggardliness

   (F) perspicacity

26. According to Darwinism, nature eliminates genetic materials that cause hereditary diseases; paradoxically, however, such lethal diseases are not as _____ as one would expect them to be.

   (A) pervasive

   (B) infrequent

   (C) ubiquitous

   (D) daunting

   (E) scarce

   (F) appalling

27. What is _____ over a dinner conversation or even on television can sometimes be broached through comedy, since it represents the one avenue where, perhaps because of its trademark facetiousness, topics can be addressed that would otherwise be avoided.

   (A) approbation

   (B) pontification

   (C) anathema

   (D) defenestration

   (E) taboo

   (F) placation

28. According to management theory, it is desirable to expect increased employee productivity if _____ investments are done in training, infrastructure, and other inputs of employee development.

   (A) commensurate

   (B) asymmetrical

   (C) zealous

   (D) proportionate

   (E) amorphous

   (F) jingoistic

29. Though some of the information the author provides about the ancient Mayan civilization may seem bizarre to us, her major themes are quite _____.

   (A) cryptic

   (B) hackneyed

   (C) soporific

   (D) bromidic

   (E) eccentric

   (F) moribund

30. After the corporate takeover and the restructuring of its policies, Delta Ware became _____: its flexible work culture replaced with bureaucracy and rigid policies.

   (A) fossilized

   (B) factious

   (C) ungovernable

   (D) ossified

   (E) schismatic

   (F) politicized

31. His parents, who were Catholics in England, had been considered _____ since they re-fused to attend the Protestant Anglican Church as required by law after the Reformation.

   (A) proletariats

   (B) patriarchs

   (C) conservatives

   (D) recusants

   (E) conformists

   (F) heretics

32. Deep and meaningful relationships are not necessarily easy, but they do allow you to be _____ and petulant sometimes, and still be loved.

   (A) cantankerous

   (B) staunch

   (C) distended

   (D) committed

   (E) curmudgeonly

   (F) credulous

33. Senator Grassley Norris, the Republican committee chairman, _____ the opposition that proposed the policies, stating that the policies are absurd and would have potentially devastating consequences, in that many people might lose their jobs, if the policies pass legislation.

    (A) persuaded

    (B) castigated

    (C) extolled

    (D) excoriated

    (E) eulogized

    (F) cajoled

34. Johanne Buhari, sworn in as Nigeria's president, remains _____: in his past administrations he had been both a proponent of democratic change and a harsh military dictator who jailed journalists, inflicted physical humiliation on civil servants and expelled thousands of immigrants.

    (A) an enigma

    (B) a tyro

    (C) a paradox

    (D) an anachronism

    (E) a paragon

    (F) a pedant

35. The jury had great difficulty forming a consensus, primarily because its members had such _____ opinions about the case.

    (A) divergent

    (B) congruous

    (C) jovial

    (D) disparate

    (E) flippant

    (F) amicable

36. MacGill, an expert in photographic compositions, points out that the subtle details captured in the photograph make it the most beautiful he has ever seen; yet to the common man, who cannot discern such subtleties, the photograph might seem quite _____.

    (A) pedestrian

    (B) prosaic

    (C) despondent

    (D) exuberant

    (E) dogmatic

    (F) doleful

37. After the advent of the Internet, people have become "speed readers": focused more on reading that is _____ rather than painstaking and absorbed.

    (A) pedantic

    (B) exacting

    (C) lingering

    (D) cursory

    (E) fastidious

    (F) perfunctory

38. Often _____, most of Wordsworth's poems may seem too melancholic to some.

    (A) hackneyed

    (B) pious

    (C) bromidic

    (D) doleful

    (E) sanctimonious

    (F) plaintive

39. While plainly advocating cuts in the military budget, the group turns to _____ when it comes to talking taxes.

    (A) vituperation

    (B) cogency

    (C) circumlocution

    (D) interrogation

    (E) euphemism

    (F) eloquence

40. This result, titled "Re-education Machine", conjures a compartmentalized, overanalyzed, possibly totalitarian environment where young minds are _____ molded.

    (A) assiduously

    (B) seductively

    (C) unstintingly

    (D) sedulously

    (E) tantalizingly

    (F) fatuously

41. Paradoxically, the spirited work of Salman Rushdie, who became famous for being issued a fatwa calling for the death by a religious leader, drew both public support and _____.

    (A) denunciation

(B)   impersonation

(C)   reprobation

(D)   commendation

(E)   adulation

(F)   imitation

42.   Industrial moguls, with billions of dollars at their disposal, are entering politics and dictating political reforms; this has raised concerns in many that we may be very close to creating _____ in this country: a state in which our country's decisions are made solely by a handful very wealthy individuals.

(A)   an oligarchy

(B)   an autocracy

(C)   a bureaucracy

(D)   an adhocracy

(E)   a plutocracy

(F)   a theocracy

43.   Incredibly successful at an early age, Zuckerberg was often considered _____ by his subordinates: he expected that his every whim to be obeyed without question.

(A)   overbearing

(B)   lubricious

(C)   insolent

(D)   flippant

(E)   imperious

(F)   foolhardy

44.   Writers, activists, and consumers shared anecdotes online testifying to why Comcast deserved the _____ title "worst company in America."

(A)   mundane

(B)   ignominious

(C)   opprobrious

(D)   terse

(E)   equivocal

(F)   laconic

45.   That she had yearned for long to visit Spain contrasted sharply with her curiously _____ first reaction.

(A)   disconsolate

(B)   ecstatic

    (C) tepid

    (D) apathetic

    (E) enraptured

    (F) sinister

46. Italian Impressionist art is now nosing its way into the art scene, where it was once considered alien and unfamiliar and found only in the homes of rich _____ who dabbled in such esoteric things.

    (A) philistines

    (B) cognoscenti

    (C) connoisseurs

    (D) initiates

    (E) lowbrows

    (F) fledglings

47. Despite the western eulogies, Djindjic will be remembered as a _____ who enriched himself by selling his country to those who had waged war against it so mercilessly only a few years earlier.

    (A) pyromaniac

    (B) quisling

    (C) chauvinist

    (D) malingerer

    (E) treasonist

    (F) skulker

48. Jillian, in contrast to her parents who were known for their resolve and tranquility in even the most trying circumstances, was considered _____ by many of her friends and family members.

    (A) introverted

    (B) phlegmatic

    (C) mercurial

    (D) mendacious

    (E) explosive

    (F) taciturn

49. The German painter is sublime, profound, and authoritative in a way that invites high-flown comparisons and invocations of art history, yet his own utterances on art would suggest that he finds such _____ repulsive, and is suspicious of anything that romanticizes the creative act.

    (A) cynicism

(B)   aggrandizement

(C)   skepticism

(D)   antipathy

(E)   apathy

(F)   hyperbole

50.   It is assumed that the austerity measures being implemented in the advanced economies to _____ their fiscal weakness may also weigh on their growth momentum.

(A)   extenuate

(B)   cull

(C)   increase

(D)   amplify

(E)   mitigate

(F)   decimate

51.   His _____ increased with every moment, and when the bell rang at about nine o'clock he felt more like a naughty and ill-tempered child than anything else.

(A)   peevishness

(B)   caprice

(C)   petulance

(D)   solemnness

(E)   sedateness

(F)   nescience

52.   Even though it is well known that children in their adolescents are impressionable, their extreme _____ at certain situations is nevertheless surprising.

(A)   gaucheness

(B)   credulity

(C)   tactlessness

(D)   disingenuousness

(E)   naiveté

(F)   artfulness

53.   His attempts to _____ her of her belief that he was insincere were futile; she remained stubborn in her opinion, obstinately insistent that he was disingenuous.

(A)   castigate

(B)   condone

(C)   excoriate

(D) disabuse

(E) undeceive

(F) exonerate

54. Although the residents of Genosha were generally considered a primarily farming community, the _____ of the residents' occupations makes such a distinction antiquated.

   (A) profitability

   (B) productivity

   (C) diversity

   (D) fecundity

   (E) heterogeneity

   (F) stability

55. _____ within state-owned companies, the banking sector and government ministries, Doanh and other critics say, has prevented a more equitable distribution of prosperity.

   (A) Chicanery

   (B) Bureaucracy

   (C) Regimentation

   (D) Unscrupulousness

   (E) Hierarchy

   (F) Regulation

56. Although the movie '*Side Effects*' has an original screenplay, it is clear why the director might have chosen it as his valedictory work: it brings together in _____ form much of what he has created over the twenty five years of his film-making career.

   (A) synoptic

   (B) curbed

   (C) restrained

   (D) investigative

   (E) précised

   (F) melodramatic

57. Because of the inundation of never-ending news cycles and our decreasing attention spans, most news reports are _____, forgotten before they're fully assimilated; therefore, for a report to have any type of permanence, it has to be particularly exceptional.

   (A) ephemeral

   (B) donnish

   (C) parochial

   (D) evanescent

(E) pedantic

(F) insular

58. Current research on developmental psychology maintains that exposure to stressful ex-
     periences as an infant is essential for normal emotional development and that these
     experiences do not herald the onset of childhood unhappiness or _____ the onset of
     teenage disquietude.

     (A) forestall

     (B) augur

     (C) foil

     (D) portend

     (E) vitiate

     (F) maculate

59. Tim Roth's solo performance was welcomed heartily by the audience, yet the show didn't
     feel authentic because his persona onstage seemed _____.

     (A) spontaneous

     (B) contrived

     (C) candid

     (D) gaudy

     (E) affected

     (F) garish

60. Mr. Berkley drew public ire for appearing at _____ camp for flood victims, which was
     set up without any real intention to bolster relief efforts but rather intended just for the
     cameras.

     (A) an evitable

     (B) a celluloid

     (C) an ersatz

     (D) a congruous

     (E) a simpatico

     (F) an exigent

61. Medicines currently operate on the notions that the yardstick of success in treating pa-
     tients is keeping them away from surgery; the medical industry, therefore, has begun ex-
     ploring treatment methods that often postpone, and sometimes even completely _____
     the need for surgery.

     (A) expedite

     (B) trivialize

    (C) obviate

    (D) vilify

    (E) forefend

    (F) precipitate

62. Nicky Romero, a popular EDM artist, in his description of his recently released album suggested that - the process of being able to truly appreciate the intricacies in his music is _____: closed to the average "enthusiast".

    (A) intuitive

    (B) elementary

    (C) unreliable

    (D) visceral

    (E) recondite

    (F) arcane

63. Some voters have been unhappy with Holland's participation in European bailouts, saying that while _____ countries are rewarded, Dutch taxpayers suffer austerity at home.

    (A) incompetent

    (B) inept

    (C) profligate

    (D) judicious

    (E) circumspect

    (F) prodigal

64. The title "engineer" has been used so broadly in the IT world that in recent times the term's meaning has become almost _____.

    (A) pejorative

    (B) indistinct

    (C) derogatory

    (D) blurred

    (E) acceptable

    (F) convenient

65. Ego and selflessness are often found in the same individual, though being diametrically different, they mutually _____ each other, and not necessarily destroy one another.

    (A) reinforce

    (B) annihilate

    (C) enhance

    (D) attenuate

(E) decimate

(F) dampen

66. Although Jolene responded in a way that did not betray any indignation, her words were not without emotion; it seemed as if she retained her composure by carefully keeping in _____ the extremes of her sentiments.

(A) limit

(B) equilibrium

(C) friction

(D) oscillation

(E) subjection

(F) equipoise

67. Ulysses by Irish writer James Joyce has several editions in the market; but they are all _____ versions: adapted to suit a predominantly family and domestic readership.

(A) censured

(B) transcribed

(C) expurgated

(D) reproofed

(E) impounded

(F) bowdlerized

68. Larger than what it appeared to be, the sculpture that was exhibited in the dark corner of the museum was _____ by the perspective.

(A) aggrandized

(B) diminished

(C) embellished

(D) substantiated

(E) dwarfed

(F) ostracized

69. The writers of *BioShock*, a famous video game, aware that interacting with a world mostly by shooting things starts to feel limiting, used this limitation to highlight that violence is _____: that people who have no option but violence are ultimately powerless.

(A) imperative

(B) edifying

(C) futile

(D) vain

(E) gratifying

    (F) inexorable

70. King Henry VIII provided generous financial support to many young scientists and was therefore rightly called a _____ of science.

    (A) disparager

    (B) champion

    (C) detractor

    (D) patron

    (E) regent

    (F) demagogue

71. The share of Americans without jobs remains unusually high and wage growth remains weak, problems that a premature rate increase could _____.

    (A) exacerbate

    (B) mollify

    (C) eliminate

    (D) aggravate

    (E) palliate

    (F) eradicate

72. The splendor and elegance at the imperial court of the Han dynasty attracted many poets who sang the praises of the emperor and his court in the form of _____, overloaded poetry full of strange similes and allusions, but with little real feeling; In contrast, the many women singers at the court, who were mostly slaves, sang poetry that was full of natural feeling, simple in language and moving in content.

    (A) grandiloquent

    (B) pithy

    (C) perfidious

    (D) laconic

    (E) pompous

    (F) duplicitous

73. Only a few ventured to _____ the character of President Menocal himself, yet his administration was vilified as corrupt and inefficient.

    (A) bespangle

    (B) asperse

    (C) demystify

    (D) endorse

    (E) obfuscate

     (F)   besmirch

74. The popular, sanitized view of dementia is that it is a rather gentle condition: sufferers are "confused", living in the past, with imaginary friends; yet it has a more _____ side in which sufferers become aggressive and more difficult to care for than the euphemistic adjective "challenging" can possibly capture.

     (A)   truculent

     (B)   eloquent

     (C)   placid

     (D)   prolix

     (E)   pugnacious

     (F)   tranquil

75. In his satirical essay '*Atheism in the 19th century*', Frederic Harrison says that in England, the classic land of mental timidity and compromise, agnosticism was almost fashionable, while atheism was treated with _____.

     (A)   obloquy

     (B)   accolade

     (C)   apathy

     (D)   approbation

     (E)   passiveness

     (F)   calumny

76. He believed that she possessed great integrity and candor; he therefore refused to consider the possibility that her statement had been _____.

     (A)   insincere

     (B)   fatuous

     (C)   facetious

     (D)   irrelevant

     (E)   inconsequential

     (F)   disingenuous

77. The book "*The Hegel reader*" has been critically acclaimed because it clarifies many of Wilhelm Friedrich Hegel's _____ philosophical concepts, which have been considered abstract by even the most perspicacious scholars.

     (A)   inscrutable

     (B)   insidious

     (C)   sophomoric

     (D)   ignominious

(E) impenetrable

(F) nugatory

78. The "look" that, famous photographer, Lauren Ashley achieved was semi-realism, which contrasted with the more artificial, made-up poses widely used in the 70s: her pictures lacked polish and had a/an _____ that captured the nonchalant spirit of her generation.

   (A) solemnity

   (B) insouciance

   (C) graveness

   (D) animosity

   (E) carefreeness

   (F) malignancy

79. Ms. Ziegelman hasn't merely pored through old cookbooks and newspapers; she also has an admirable ability to pluck the most _____ details from them.

   (A) piquant

   (B) acrimonious

   (C) tedious

   (D) scathing

   (E) vivifying

   (F) monotonous

80. Jacques is known for his _____ collection, which showcases a varied mix of antique furniture, vintage clothing and jewelry, also specializes in French pieces from the 1940s.

   (A) banal

   (B) eclectic

   (C) baroque

   (D) refulgent

   (E) corpulent

   (F) catholic

81. Krugman points out that worries about increasing inflation rates are unfounded: not only has inflation been _____ for years, there's almost no chance it will return anytime soon.

   (A) rampant

   (B) prestigious

   (C) ineluctable

   (D) quiescent

(E)   pervasive

(F)   dormant

82.   He was modest yet certain about his talents, anxious yet cool about his reputation, and somehow both _____ and effusive about his influences.

(A)   demure

(B)   enthralled

(C)   overt

(D)   reserved

(E)   conspicuous

(F)   enraptured

83.   While the people of Turkey look forward to democratization and election of the new president, they fear that if he wins he will appoint a pliant prime minister he can control, and concentrate all true power in his own hands; technically making himself a/an _____.

(A)   demagogue

(B)   libertine

(C)   despot

(D)   autocrat

(E)   connoisseur

(F)   hedonist

84.   They wanted a tame and amenable Secretary of Defense, and they got one, but over time he became less _____, and started to push for more resources and perhaps had other differences.

(A)   indignant

(B)   pliant

(C)   recalcitrant

(D)   malleable

(E)   refractory

(F)   chivalrous

85.   The concession was a signal moment in an especially _____ campaign marked by deeply personal allegations and renewed divisions among Kentucky Republicans.

(A)   gratifying

(B)   rancorous

(C)   endearing

(D)   ardent

(E) acrimonious

(F) impassioned

86. In the series *"Room Mates"*, Solomon is recognizably a late bloomer and a bit socially _____, but this very quality is portrayed in a way that seems completely charming and never like a bad thing.

(A) gauche

(B) chipper

(C) suave

(D) adept

(E) inept

(F) debonair

87. Although his actions were perceived as _____ during his time, many after his death celebrated Guy Fawkes as a hero and a revolutionary.

(A) benevolent

(B) nefarious

(C) reprehensible

(D) salubrious

(E) sincere

(F) jocular

88. Even though the common perception is that a promotion _____ a raise in salary, this is not always the case: many professionals take on a bigger title, more responsibility, even a bigger team without a commensurate increase in compensation.

(A) jeopardizes

(B) obviates

(C) entails

(D) procrastinates

(E) engenders

(F) circumvents

89. Henry III's dreams of autocracy at home and far-reaching dominion abroad were _____ in a century of constitutional ideas and national differentiation; this earned the contempt of Englishmen and foreigners alike by the instability of his purpose.

(A) anachronistic

(B) avant-garde

(C) egalitarian

(D) antiquated

    (E) visionary

    (F) populist

90. Survey pilots must fly exact grids over their assigned areas, maintaining their target altitude and ground speed, sometimes through _____ winds and weather.

    (A) fickle

    (B) clement

    (C) trivial

    (D) inconsequential

    (E) mercurial

    (F) serene

91. The Bulgarians denounced the Servians as _____ and faithless and the Servians responded by excoriating the colossal greed and intolerance of the Bulgarians.

    (A) perfidious

    (B) laconic

    (C) solemn

    (D) terse

    (E) craven

    (F) austere

92. Jeff Bercovici, after his frivolous remark about AIDS, publicly apologized for his faux pas and said that even though we read about its devastating effects on the news, it is terribly easy to be _____ about an epidemic that one has never witnessed firsthand.

    (A) colloquial

    (B) cognizant

    (C) cavalier

    (D) tangential

    (E) tactful

    (F) offhand

93. Taylor Huff calls tourists who partake in the trend of attaching locks to public places, to express their "affection" for their loved ones selfish, but reserves her greatest scorn and _____ for American celebrities photographed attaching locks to the bridge.

    (A) opprobrium

    (B) obloquy

    (C) blandishments

    (D) piety

    (E) plaudits

   (F) priggishness

94. Fun-loving Peter Russel's seemingly nonsensical jokes aimed at some weird cultural prac-
    tices of a certain community, took a/an _____ turn at the end, leaving the
    audience disconcerted and fazed.

    (A) edifying

    (B) squeamish

    (C) woozy

    (D) preaching

    (E) soothing

    (F) uncanny

95. The captain's masterstroke of the inclusion of five bowlers in the team, yielded results
    as surprising as they were promising; his next move was to leverage on the asset that
    would _____ his unpopular decision.

    (A) corroborate

    (B) contravene

    (C) abjure

    (D) plough

    (E) upbear

    (F) burlesque

96. The strained diplomatic ties between North Korea and South Korea are _____
    enough that despite external intervention it may lead to cataclysm.

    (A) quixotic

    (B) turbulent

    (C) volatile

    (D) superfluous

    (E) pecuniary

    (F) inundated

97. British fictional secret service agent James Bonds' unrelenting success to _____
    opponents' hide-outs has inspired many movie-makers to make similar spy movies,
    which involve a sleuthing protagonist who ultimately sabotages the diabolic plans of
    a devious villain.

    (A) estrange

    (B) foil

    (C) intrude

    (D) invade

(E) flinch

(F) inundate

98. The reality is that corruption has been _____ for a while, and that it can hardly be assumed to have been surmounted; let the national election be over and corruption will run rampant as it did before.

(A) languished

(B) crippled

(C) stagnant

(D) escalating

(E) quiescent

(F) regurgitating

99. George appears _____; yet, his show of seemingly uncanny wisdom in a bid to solve a complex problem soon received grimacing responses from the grade students.

(A) tyro

(B) neophyte

(C) greenhorn

(D) rustic

(E) dexterous

(F) adroit

100. Though for a westerner, the difference between One-Day form of Cricket (most popular game in the sub-continent regions) and its T-20 form is trifling, for a person of the sub-continent regions, it is _____.

(A) synoptic

(B) null and void

(C) crucial

(D) immense

(E) optional

(F) nominal

Chapter 4

Concepts of Text Completion

Text Completion questions are formed out of a sentence or sentences with one, two, or three blanks; each blank can be filled with a word or a phrase, which makes a meaningful sentence or paragraph in context. Single-blank Text Completion questions are very similar to Sentence Equivalence questions but, unlike Sentence Equivalence questions, have only five options, of which only one is correct.

Let us see the example of a single-blank TC question:

Never known to be a master of pretense, Tom was a standing testimony to _____; even a blatant masquerade of humility was presented with poise.
ingenuity
peevishness
magnanimity
affectation
enunciation

In the GRE examination, options are not marked with A, B, C, D, E, & F, rather they are arranged in columns. Though the GRE uses circular radio buttons for questions with one correct answer, for Text Completion (TC) questions, it asks you to click the option word(s); upon clicking, the selected word or phrase is highlighted and your selection is registered.

Since it is cumbersome to refer to options without their short references–A, B, C, D, E, & F, we will list options through alphabetized list. So, in the book you will find the options listed as below.

A.	ingenuity
B.	peevishness
C.	magnanimity
D.	affectation
E.	enunciation

Let us see the example of a two-blank TC question:

Punctured Equilibrium views Darwinian gene flows and causation to be overly (i) _____ or simplistic. In actuality, say its proponents, any comparative advantage acquired by the member of a species would, under most conditions, be re-absorbed and 'averaged out' among a sizable number of members of the species before it had time to be visible, a gradation too (ii) _____ for Darwin and his naturalists to observe.

Blank (i)	Blank (ii)
A. manipulative	D. underhanded
B. ambitious	E. elusive
C. meticulous	F. cantankerous

It is to be noted that the options listed in the first column of the option table, named Blank (i) are meant for the first blank in the question, this follows that the options listed in the second column, named Blank (ii) are meant for the second blank.

It is to be noted that in order to get the credit for the question, you must select the correct answer for each blank. This means that if you selected the correct option for Blank (i) and incorrect option for Blank (ii), or vice-versa, you will not get the credit for the question.

We see that considering all the combinations, your chance to get a two-blank question right is 1 out of 9! Still better that a SE question, for which your chance of getting a question right is 1 out of 15; however, this comparison isn't practical since both question types are a little different in the approaches needed to solve them.

Let us see the example of a three-blank TC question:

It has been witnessed that the opposition vindicates its _____ demeanor in the National Assembly, because quite often the ruling party, the then opposition used to put the Assembly on _____. However, two minuses cannot help _____ the ledger of the country.

Blank (i)	Blank (ii)	Blank (iii)
A. higgledy-piggledy	D. anabasis	G. cark
B. wishy-washy	E. stalemate	H. equipoise
C. abominable	F. mesa	I. equivocate

Quite often you would find that for two- and three-blank questions (occasionally for single-blank questions), the question provides more than one sentence; like in this question, you are provided with two sentences. Mathematically speaking, though, your chance to get a three-blank question right is 1 out of 27, there may be a three-blank question which is easier than a two-blank or a single-blank question; it depends on what kinds of sentence(s) the question provides and the hardness level of vocabulary used in the options.

Like SE questions, TC questions also ask you to...

- Understand the meaning of the sentence(s) from the partial information.

- Understand the logical structure of the sentence(s).

- Understand hint or clue words or phrases.

- Understand the role of transition or signal word(s), such as, moreover, though, but, etc.

- Understand the contextual meanings of option words.

Let us take the example and develop the approach to solve single-blank TC questions.

The approach to solve single-blank TC questions is similar to that required to solve SE questions, except that you need not look for a near-synonym pair and that you only need to select a single option for a blank.

Never known to be a master of pretense, Tom was a standing testimony to _____; even a blatant masquerade of humility was presented with poise.

A.	ingenuity
B.	peevishness
C.	magnanimity
D.	affectation
E.	enunciation

This question type falls under the category of medium to hard questions as the words are slightly complex and an average test taker may not know the meanings of all the words. A better approach is to break down the sentence and focus on the words you know. This way you can get a hang of the question.

Let us try to understand the meaning of the sentence from the partial information.

This sentence is dense: it has many words typically tested on the GRE, such as testimony, blatant, masquerade, and poise. The sentence describes Tom and his previous nature of not being a master of pretense - one who pretends or fakes. Later on, he became a testimony (evidence, demonstration) to **something** and presented a blatant (obvious; clear) masquerade (pretense; disguise) of humility, with poise (composure, coolness).

If we work out from the known part of the sentence, we can infer that Tom presented humility with poise. You can assume poise to be calmness or balance that is required to present something. And why was there a need to present humility? That means it's not coming out naturally and he was fabricating/faking it. Thus, the blank has to take a word with a negative connotation, and should be a synonym to fabrication. So, a suggestive **fill-in** is **fabrication.**

The **hint-phrase** is **even a blatant...something of humility was presented with poise** and **signal words** – **'pretense' and 'poise'** further help to understand the **fill-in**.

Let us pre-empt the **fill-in**; it should be negative and relatable words from the synonym family of **fabrication**.

Let us understand the meanings of the option words from the blank.

   A. ingenuity – cleverness; skill

   B. peevishness – irritability; fussiness

   C. magnanimity – generosity; lavishness

   D. affectation – artificiality; insincerity

   E. enunciation – diction; articulation

The correct answer would be 'affectation'. While 'ingenuity' would have been a close call, it's more of a positive word and used in a general context. Though 'peevishness' is negative in the context, the meaning of irritability does not match the required context. The other words are not relevant in the context.

The correct answer is 'affectation'.

Let us take the example and develop the approach to solve two-blank TC questions.

Punctured Equilibrium views Darwinian gene flows and causation to be overly (i) _____ or simplistic. In actuality, say its proponents, any comparative advantage acquired by the member of a species would, under most conditions, be re-absorbed and 'averaged out' among a sizable number of members of the species before it had time to be visible, a gradation too (ii) _____ for Darwin and his naturalists to observe.

Blank (i)		Blank (ii)	
A.	manipulative	D.	underhanded
B.	ambitious	E.	elusive
C.	meticulous	F.	cantankerous

This question type falls under the category of medium to hard questions as the topic or the content of the question is slightly complex; moreover the length of the text also makes this question a challenging one. A better approach is to break down the sentence and focus on the words you know. This way you can get a hang of the question.

With the mention of 'Punctured Equilibrium', it may seem as though GRE through its SE/TC questions requires a bit of outside knowledge; however this is not the case. If you replace 'Punctured Equilibrium' with some kind of theory or simply 'PE theory', the understanding of the text will not be affected.

It is expected that you know about Darwin and his theory of genes (you are not expected to master it), understanding of species, and basic functions of genes.

Let us understand the meanings of the sentences from the partial information.

The first sentence is a viewpoint of Punctured Equilibrium theory on 'Darwinian gene flows and causation'. PE describes 'Darwinian gene flows and causation' as overly **something (fill-in 1)**, or simplistic. If one only reads the first sentence, he or she may seek for relatable adjectives from the synonym family of **simplistic** (naïve; unilateral; myopic). However, it seems that followed by the first sentence, a lengthy 4-line sentence describes the characteristics of 'Darwinian gene flows and causation', and we would get a hint for **fill-in 1.**

Since the second sentence starts with a **signal word** – 'In actuality', we can sense that PE proponents would have a contrasting viewpoint for 'Darwinian gene flows and causation' theory.

In simpler terms, PE proponents contests that if a member of a species, say for example, a particular monkey from the primate species evolves in it a characteristic that other members of its species do not possess, the differentiated characteristic will pass on to other members (here, monkeys). Subsequently, the anticipated change in the very monkey will not be visible or noticed. PE proponents counter that the degree of change or the gradation would be too **something (fill-in 2)** to observe.

It is much easier to pre-empt **fill-in 2** than **fill-in 1**; **fill-in 2** should be relatable adjectives from the synonym family of **subtle**.

Let us understand the meanings of the option words from blank (ii).

   D. underhanded – deceitful; sneaky

   E. elusive – subtle; refined

   F. cantankerous – complaining; unreasonable

The correct answer for blank (ii) would be 'elusive'. The words 'underhanded' and 'cantankerous' do not fit the context of the sentence.

Let us pre-empt **fill-in 1**. Since PE proponents contrast Darwin's theory and describe the perceptible change as one that is difficult to observe or notice, **fill-in 1** should be relatable words from the synonym family of **simplistic**.

Let us understand the meanings of the option words from blank (i).

   A. manipulative – devious; controlling

   B. ambitious – aspiring; striving

   C. meticulous – particular; scrupulous

We do not find any suitable relatable words from the synonym family of **simplistic**. In such a scenario, it is advisable that we must pick the word that suits most in the context. Since PE proponents contrast Darwin's theory and its unrealistic postulates, it may describe Darwin's theory as overly **ambitious**. The correct answer for blank (i) would be 'ambitious'.

The correct answers are 'ambitious' & 'elusive'.

Let us take the example and develop the approach to solve three-blank TC questions.

It has been witnessed that the opposition vindicates its _____ demeanor in the National Assembly, because quite often the ruling party, the then opposition used to put the Assembly on _____. However, two minuses cannot help _____ the ledger of the country.

	Blank (i)		Blank (ii)		Blank (iii)
A.	higgledy-piggledy	D.	anabasis	G.	cark
B.	wishy-washy	E.	stalemate	H.	equipoise
C.	abominable	F.	mesa	I.	equivocate

This question type falls under the category of medium to hard questions as the words are slightly complex and an average test taker may not know the meanings of all the words. The text is stylistically different from normal texts which you would often see in typical questions. Ending the question text with *"However, two minuses cannot help _____ the ledger of the country,"* the test maker leaves something for you to infer. Again a better approach is to break down the sentence and focus on the words you know. This way you can get a hang of the question.

Let us understand the meanings of the sentences from the partial information.

The sentences states that the opposition justifies its **some kind of** behavior in the National Assembly, because it argues that quite often the ruling party, when it was in the opposition, used to hold the Assembly on **something**. The second sentence starts with a **signal word** – 'however', which implies that the opposing thought is going to follow. It says that however two minuses (infer it as 'two wrong acts') cannot make **something** the ledger (record) of the country.

Let us pre-empt the **fill-ins**.

fill-in 3 is the easiest to pre-empt. It should be relatable words from the synonyms family of **'balance'**.

Let us understand the meanings of the option words from the blanks (iii).

   G. cark – to burden or be burdened with trouble; worry

   H. equipoise – to equal or offset; balance

   I. equivocate – to fudge; beat around the bush

The correct answer is 'equipoise'. While 'cark' is nearly opposite of what we need, 'equivocate' is not relevant in the context.

It is logical to conclude that **fill-in 1** and **fill-in 2** should be in sync with each other as the opposition justifies its behavior because it argues that the ruling party also did the same in the past; moreover **fill-in 1** and **fill-in 2** must be negative words.

Let us understand the meanings of the option words from the blanks (i).

   A. higgledy-piggledy – disorderly; unruly

   B. wishy-washy – weak; spineless

   C. abominable – detestable; horrible

The correct answer is 'higgledy-piggledy'. The opposition would not like to justify its wishy-washy (feeble) behavior in the backdrop of the then opposition's outrageous behavior. In the same vein, the opposition would not like to be looked at as a party whose behavior is abominable (horrible).

Let us understand the meanings of the option words from the blanks (ii).

   D. anabasis – a forward path; expedition

   E. stalemate – impasse; logjam

   F. mesa – peak; plateau

The correct answer is 'stalemate'. While 'anabasis' is opposite of what we need, 'mesa' is not relevant.

The correct answers are 'higgledy-piggledy', 'stalemate', & 'equipoise'.

Process of solving TC questions

The process of solving Text Completion questions is largely the same as that of Sentence Equivalence questions. You must have seen following steps earlier in SE concept, but we have reproduced the same with few revisions, applicable to TC questions.

(1) Understand the meaning(s) of the sentence(s) from the partial information

(2) Understand the role of transition/signal word(s)

> Whether the transition/signal word(s) carries the thought in the same direction or in the opposite direction

(3) Relate hint word(s) or phrase(s) with signal word(s) to pre-empt the fill-ins.

(4) Pre-empt the fill-in word(s) or phrase(s)

> (a) Understand the tone of the sentence(s)
>
> > Test-maker may cleverly craft a sarcastic sentence that may seemingly ask for a fill-in word, which has a positive undertone, however the correct fill-in word should have a negative undertone and vice-versa
>
> (b) Be sure to have contextually relatable near-synonym words for pre-empt word(s) or phrase(s)

(5) Understand the meanings of the option words

> (a) Keeping in mind contextually in the mind, for each blank, select an option word that is best suited for the pre-empt word(s) or phrase(s)
>
> (b) If you do not know the meanings of all the option words, you may apply process of elimination. Though it seems simple, it is not easy. The key is to learn vocabulary! We will have a separate book for vocabulary.
>
> (c) In case of two- and three-blank questions, assure that each selection is in sync with the other(s). Re-read the question sentence(s) with selected options and reassure that the question text as a whole makes sense.

In the next chapter, you will find 100 Text Completion questions for practice.

Chapter 5

Text Completion Questions

1-blank TC questions

1. In America, turkey, otherwise known as turducken, is the most popular food by several orders of eminence, whereas in Europe, Danish meatballs are evenly _____ among a few varied foods.

A.	distributed
B.	qualified
C.	viewed
D.	influenced
E.	noted

2. The neuroscientist argues that our journals and videos about stem cell therapy are a way of mass _____ and that only a stroke of luck hitherto unobserved could allow a human being to even venture to reproduce a new brain.

A.	insanity
B.	newness
C.	hallucination
D.	frenzy
E.	cataclysm

3. In a research conducted in 1980, an argument presupposed that the probability of using mobile phones for calling was as likely as residing in Mars, an argument that today sounds _____.

A.	nescient
B.	succinct
C.	indolent
D.	outmoded
E.	incredulous

4. Da Vinci is of course most famous for his artistic brilliance, but his novel designs of a flying machine had an understated but more _____ impact, as his principles strongly influenced aircraft design well into the 21st century.

A.	indelible
B.	laudatory
C.	ephemeral
D.	indigent
E.	filial

5. Though retired, the scientist makes an effort to remain _____ the newest research in his field.

A.	enchanted by
B.	astounded by
C.	cognizant of
D.	apathetic to
E.	taken aback by

6. January's Tsunami was but a _____ to a dreadful year that brought about a barrage of terrifying plagues, natural calamities, and economic devastations to the small island of Nauru.

A.	expurgation
B.	prelude
C.	orgy
D.	prolegomenon
E.	monologue

7. Following a short-lived squabble over decision-making, the team chose a leader and _____ into a strikingly congenial group.

A.	collocated
B.	mangled
C.	shriveled
D.	commingled
E.	appropriated

8. The writer, in his re-adaptation of a play set in the 16th Century, added studied _____ into the movie - for example, Shylock used a calculator to add the interest and the principal.

A.	vapidity
B.	shibboleth
C.	rigmarole
D.	metachronism
E.	inferences

9. Chavez, a tyrannical ruler and the despot who had committed several human rights violations against his own people, in his interview came off as surprisingly _____; this could explain why such reprehensible rulers are able to gain the loyalties of so many of their subjects.

A.	magnanimous
B.	malignant
C.	austere
D.	draconian
E.	grandiose

10. Much of what the public came to believe about the Columbine high school shootings was flat-out wrong. Myths took root from the start, nurtured by frightened and confused students and amplified by news outlets running hard with rumor and _____.

A.	serendipity
B.	travesty
C.	certitude
D.	conjecture
E.	iniquity

11. It is a common phenomenon that most students, who actively participate in extracurricular activities, do not have much trouble getting recognition during their school and college days; yet, when they graduate and enter adulthood they are _____ relative obscurity in their work environments.

A.	spent on
B.	satiated with
C.	regaled with
D.	relegated to
E.	pacified with

12. Biologists tend to eliminate rather than revise pre-Darwinian theories about evolution, thereby _____ not only their uniqueness, but their very existence.

A.	contesting
B.	extolling
C.	explaining
D.	transfiguring
E.	anticipating

13. For months, Russian officials and television networks have painted the revolutionaries as a fascist _____, intent on stripping ethnic Russians of their rights.

A.	encomium
B.	regime
C.	reform
D.	cabal
E.	leadership

14. Though archaeologists are always portrayed digging for artifacts in uninhabited deserts, most of their research actually happen in libraries, where most of their discoveries are _____ by pouring through volumes of research textbooks.

A.	emblazoned
B.	perused
C.	absconded
D.	incited
E.	circumscribed

15. The problem with Bernie is that he delivers too many long and bombastic speeches on his campaign trail; this makes him come off as _____ rather than eloquent.

A.	glib
B.	fatuous
C.	loquacious
D.	unscrupulous
E.	taciturn

16. In his book 'Why winners quit', author James Samaritan _____ those who stick to a single employer for the entire of their career, pointing out that on average, almost all competent workers change jobs at least once every three years.

A.	chides
B.	approbates
C.	immolates
D.	placates
E.	censors

17. After receiving several complaints from students that he, almost too eagerly, gave out _____ criticism, the professor was asked by the management to adhere to a more diplomatic approach while dealing with students.

A.	nondescript
B.	scathing
C.	insipid
D.	subtle
E.	judicious

18. The recent economic crisis that propagated intense job cutbacks and a recession in many industries has created a/an _____ job market; as a result many young adults opt to continue their education rather than try to compete for the few available jobs.

A.	salubrious
B.	decadent
C.	anemic
D.	facile
E.	malignant

19. In ancient Greece, young men would often seek out philosophical mentors to guide them through their philosophical and spiritual journeys; but, when a teacher or guru tries to guide a young man who does not seek out mentoring, the gesture generally comes off as patronizing and _____.

A.	affable
B.	pastoral
C.	sententious
D.	torrential
E.	salubrious

20. Interested in being creative and innovative, and always wanting to do something new, _____ always tend to look at situations from a different angle than would people in general do.

A.	idolaters
B.	initiates
C.	sociopaths
D.	mavericks
E.	mendicants

21. Mr. Macintyre himself writes about spies so craftily, and so _____, that you half suspect him of being some type of spook.

A.	tortuously
B.	surreptitiously
C.	apathetically
D.	ebulliently
E.	insipidly

22. The previous CEO, who was known for his aggressive tactics and hostility toward competition, created a lot of antagonists in the tech industry. In contrast, his _____ successor has helped repair relationships with rivaling firms to create a more nurturing ecosystem in the tech industry.

A.	emollient
B.	repugnant
C.	sophomoric
D.	peripatetic
E.	indigent

23. The interview was deeply unpleasant, with a windy, _____ subject who answered almost every question in 15-minute soliloquies, many of which were not particularly useful.

A.	brawny
B.	parsimonious
C.	laconic
D.	fraternal
E.	refractory

24. Biologists have incontrovertible evidence that proves that there are no free-living creatures that live in complete solitude; this makes the point that life is _____ other forms.

A.	isolated from
B.	dependent on
C.	foregrounded by
D.	antithetical to
E.	emulated by

25. Amelia's speech sparked a lot of disagreement, yet, even those who disagreed with her views rarely faulted her for expressing them because the positions she took were as _____ as they were tendentious.

A.	reflective
B.	political
C.	recondite
D.	impractical
E.	banal

26. Even after hours of deliberation, the members of the evaluation team could not develop a consensus on who the winning candidate will be, primarily because the criteria for evaluation of various members of the evaluation team rested on such _____ preferences.

A.	trite
B.	trifling
C.	obvious
D.	divergent
E.	antiquated

27. Celina, in contrast to her parents who were known for their resolve and tranquility in even the most trying of circumstances, was considered _____ by many of her friends and family members.

A.	placid
B.	introverted
C.	mercurial
D.	mendacious
E.	taciturn

28. Her essays about communism and antagonistic reforms were initially met with hostility by reviewers, and although their opinions softened with time, only a few reviewers now _____ her essays.

A.	celebrate
B.	revile
C.	criticize
D.	neglect
E.	scrutinize

29. As seen in the *Da Vinci code*, The Holy Grail puts forward a real _____: one that led powerful men go on a blind trail and commit a series of heinous crimes but in the end, no one was able to decipher.

A.	impasse
B.	verse
C.	treasure
D.	commensuration
E.	dilemma

30. Nancy's fable, which to a casual reader appears to be an uncomplicated story of children visiting a museum, takes a/an _____ turn in the end, warning people to always be cautious.

A.	benevolent
B.	apathetic
C.	candid
D.	pugnacious
E.	sententious

31. The editor of the news channel's "Debate Hour" remarked that it was difficult to find an appropriate arbitrator for certain disputatious matters, as nobody is _____ with regards to these issues.

A.	convivial
B.	facetious
C.	dispassionate
D.	equivocal
E.	frivolous

32. The CEO's team members maintained that he had never taken an injudicious decision during the crisis, but the CEO dispelled this as _____, taking it as the mealy-mouthed garrulity of sycophants.

A.	treachery
B.	impecuniousness
C.	toadyism
D.	banter
E.	mimicry

33. The illusive modesty of a silk dress _____ the staggering hours of hard work required to produce silk; from rearing the silkworms to harvesting them under exacting requirements.

A.	certifies
B.	remodels
C.	endows
D.	belies
E.	impedes

34. With so many multiplexes shutting down due to economic downturn, students might just have to return to their books as there will not be any accessible places to be _____ around in.

A.	scaling
B.	loafing
C.	philandering
D.	apportioning
E.	excogitating

35. The risk of using a deluge of media and TV ad campaigns to promote sponsorship is that it can make the NGO that utilizes it look _____ rather than upright.

A.	meticulous
B.	magniloquent
C.	disingenuous
D.	insipid
E.	articulate

36. In the last decade, gun violence in schools has become so _____ that schools now mandate routine drills, in which students run for cover and are taught evasive measures if they come in close proximity to the killer.

A.	ubiquitous
B.	perfunctory
C.	iconoclastic
D.	prosaic
E.	refulgent

37. The latest science fiction novel set in 2300 AD, which generated a lot of hype because of the advertising efforts by the publisher, was not so enthusiastically received by the critics; one of the critics is quoted to have said that, though the book does contain some pioneering ideas, it could hardly be called _____.

A.	orthodox
B.	radical
C.	eccentric
D.	trivial
E.	controversial

38. As far back as the Industrial Revolution, there have been periodic panics about the impact of automation. Handloom weavers' resistance to new machines earned them the pejorative title of _____ that has become a byword for all those who try in vain to stop technological progress.

A.	patriarchs
B.	racists
C.	egalitarians
D.	elitists
E.	luddites

39. It has been found that students, who are quite independent and self-sufficient, take care of their own learning needs; these students benefit most from the _____ of constant teacher-student mentoring, which other students require.

A.	revitalization
B.	legislation
C.	elimination
D.	concretization
E.	sublimation

40. Though advances in inoculation have been substantial in the past century, there are still _____ infant deaths each year caused by diseases that are purportedly preventable.

A.	marginal
B.	fortuitous
C.	equitable
D.	significant
E.	modest

41. Following the recent outbreak of mad-cow disease in Malaysia, its neighbor -Singapore recommended its domestic food regulation department to shift from cursory checks of farm animals to a more _____ sampling for the presence of the bovine infection.

A.	superficial
B.	perfunctory
C.	rigorous
D.	solicitous
E.	synergetic

42. Ironically, the tirade intended to correct the insolence in the cadet, served only to _____ his disrespectful ways.

A.	turn him away from
B.	absolve him from
C.	reinforce
D.	obfuscate
E.	extenuate

43. A manhunt is under way for a patient who _____ from a psychiatric hospital in south-east London after assaulting two members of staff.

A.	jettisoned
B.	absconded
C.	arrogated
D.	proliferated
E.	squabbled

44. While most of us are probably familiar with the feel-good effect of helping others, when you are sick, that _____ takes on new meaning; it transmutes from being merely a good feeling to becoming a therapeutic treatment that heals your own illnesses.

A.	infirmity
B.	circumspection
C.	magnanimity
D.	malevolence
E.	garrulity

45. Proponents of biometric security system argue that biometric security system is inherently more secure because fingerprints are a/an _____ physical attribute that can't be altered by criminals.

A.	immutable
B.	amorphous
C.	superficial
D.	ephemeral
E.	picturesque

46. That the artist has the ability to strike a/an _____ between the abstract and the real in his street paintings, creating an almost surreal contrast in them, is one of the things that drew Martin to Harris' work.

A.	imposture
B.	harmony
C.	dichotomy
D.	equipoise
E.	serenade

47. Athleticism and a _____ temperament are a sought-after combination of traits in horses; they are the underpinnings of a successful equine competitor.

A.	rancorous
B.	dispassionate
C.	nonchalant
D.	hubristic
E.	tractable

48. Appearing on NBC, Rick Perry, the key spokesperson of Republican Party, _____ Trump's criticism of his record on border security and said: "Trump does not represent the Republican party".

A.	pacified
B.	anthropomorphized
C.	eulogized
D.	exsanguinated
E.	repudiated

49. They profess that they know God, but by their works they deny him, being abominable and disobedient, and unto every good work _____.

A.	amicable
B.	sanguine
C.	fictitious
D.	reprobate
E.	felicitous

50. Although unknown in the world of rugby, the Japanese rugby team with its sensational win last year was brought to the spotlight; and suddenly, rugby, a _____ sport in a country where baseball, soccer, and sumo dominate, is in vogue.

A.	querulous
B.	pompous
C.	niche
D.	commonplace
E.	reprehensible

2-blanks TC questions

51. Scientists have, so far, only been able to speculate as to why animal species did not (i) _____ sooner even though offshoots had long started (ii) _____, once ample oxygen enveloped the Earth's surface.

Blank (i)	Blank (ii)
A. vanish	D. emulsifying
B. emblematize	E. vanishing
C. burgeon	F. sprouting

52. Contingency theory asserts that managers make decisions based on the situation at hand rather than a "one size fits all" method. While a leader in the army may exercise a _____ leadership approach for a problem, a manager in a university may embrace a _____ leadership approach for the same problem.

Blank (i)	Blank (ii)
A. despotic	D. transphobic
B. participative	E. tyrannical
C. luscious	F. parching

53. In her workplace, Jemima's (i) _____ is often mistaken for (ii) _____; her close-friends, however, have become accustomed to her habit of being brutally honest.

Blank (i)	Blank (ii)
A. torpor	D. acrimony
B. candor	E. modesty
C. hubris	F. complacence

54. Since 1930, reaction to the theories of psychoanalysis by Sigmund Freud has fluctuated between adoration and (i) _____; but in general, later psychoanalysts have esteemed his works more highly than did most of his (ii) _____.

Blank (i)	Blank (ii)
A. peregrination	D. progenitors
B. condescension	E. archetypes
C. veneration	F. contemporaries

55. Given that the works of earlier poets, such as, Walt Whitman and T.S. Eliot (i) _____ Harold Bloom, it would be incorrect to view his works as entirely (ii) _____ creations.

Blank (i)	Blank (ii)
A. were inspired by	D. calumnious
B. had an influence on	E. independent
C. were antithetical with	F. collaborative

56. Prior to the work of Philip, illustrations of geographic features were often beautiful but rarely (i) _____; this fact, combined with the (ii) _____ nature of most 18th century geographic descriptions, often kept researchers from identifying nuances in geographical entities.

Blank (i)	Blank (ii)
A. traditional	D. inexact
B. divisive	E. reformist
C. precise	F. expatiated

57. For the ardent fans of the actor, his life seems to be a paradox of sorts. The (i) _____ characters portrayed by him on screen are a stark contrast to his utterly (ii) _____ lifestyle.

Blank (i)	Blank (ii)
A. obscure	D. colorful
B. flamboyant	E. mawkish
C. affluent	F. vapid

58. As the first commercial airplane to reach supersonic speeds, the Concorde represented a (i) _____ in the aviation industry, and although initial acceptance by commuters was (ii) _____, it had an immense influence on the luxury transportation industry.

Blank (i)	Blank (ii)
A. milestone	D. prodigious
B. regression	E. disappointing
C. cornerstone	F. trifling

59. John Gladstone is the leading expert in turning (i) _____ things into (ii) _____ events. His annual 'Gladstone Report' is a glowing example of how seemingly mundane information can tell a beautiful story with just a little artistic treatment.

Blank (i)	Blank (ii)
A. inauspicious	D. picayune
B. quotidian	E. banal
C. propitious	F. mesmerizing

60. That she was (i) _____ swimming did not diminish her (ii) _____ to join her friends on a scuba diving trip.

Blank (i)	Blank (ii)
A. attracted to	D. determination
B. fearful of	E. reluctance
C. knowledgeable	F. about reservedness

61. For her efforts to revitalize the economic systems of the indigent communities, Martha has quite (i) _____ become the object of both great contempt and great (ii) _____.

Blank (i)	Blank (ii)
A. paradoxically	D. veneration
B. predictably	E. befuddlement
C. ostensibly	F. placation

62. The theology of the Westborough Baptist Church, while tolerant to those of other denominations, is (i) _____ to what it regards (ii) _____.

Blank (i)	Blank (ii)
A. unapologetically indifferent	D. refulgent
B. unstintingly forgiving	E. heterodox
C. uncompromisingly hostile	F. supercilious

63. Georgia was (i) _____ by nature: she preferred to speak only when absolutely necessary and therefore found Jake's relentless chatter completely (ii) _____.

Blank (i)	Blank (ii)
A. ebullience	D. discomfiting
B. laconic	E. enchanting
C. asocial	F. stimulating

64. Most people in many Asian countries consider the words of their mentors (i) _____: to doubt them is considered almost (ii) _____.

Blank (i)	Blank (ii)
A. incontrovertible	D. sacrilegious
B. inevitable	E. reverential
C. excruciating	F. felicitous

65. Though most of the people in the audience were adults, they were filled with a sense of (i) _____ as they watched the movie *Growing Up*, a movie that has been acclaimed for portraying the experiences and emotions of teenage life very realistically and (ii) _____.

Blank (i)	Blank (ii)
A. animosity	D. banally
B. nostalgia	E. evocatively
C. ennui	F. sterilely

66. Charles, well known for his (i) _____, (ii) _____ no open disagreement from any of his subordinates once he had made a decision.

Blank (i)	Blank (ii)
A. impetuousness	D. brooked
B. imperiousness	E. dispatched
C. equipoise	F. condescended

67. The Jackson family was known for not giving into (i) _____. None of the family memebers feared (ii) _____: of acting and being different from their neighbors.

Blank (i)	Blank (ii)
A. sensibility	D. adulation
B. humility	E. insubordination
C. conformity	F. singularity

68. That fundamentalism in religion destroys scientific progress appears to be corroborated by evidence through history: scientific progress has (i) _____ only when fundamentalist religious beliefs have been (ii) _____.

Blank (i)	Blank (ii)
A. pandered	D. neglected
B. flourished	E. promoted
C. fulminated	F. patronized

69. Although behaviorists have established fairly clear (i) _____ that describe appropriate behavior of animals; there seems to be (ii) _____ about what constitutes appropriate behavior for humans.

Blank (i)	Blank (ii)
A. norms	D. certainty
B. obfuscations	E. confusion
C. conundrums	F. rigidity

70. The press release about the new version of the gaming console, and its proposed release next fall, posed an unexpected problem for Atari Gaming Corporation. People were so excited about the new (i) _____ of the console that they refused to purchase the (ii) _____ version.

Blank (i)	Blank (ii)
A. iteration	D. outmoded
B. stereotype	E. prevailing
C. legacy	F. parochial

71. Unfortunately, Nikola Tesla, who is (i) _____ as one of the most prodigious minds, was (ii) _____, during his time, as a man who was not sufficiently educated to make the scientific breakthroughs that he did.

Blank (i)	Blank (ii)
A. ostracized	D. deified
B. vilified	E. glorified
C. venerated	F. dismissed

72. While he faced criticism for his intervention in Syria in the past, President Obama is now facing (i) _____for his (ii) _____ it.

Blank (i)	Blank (ii)
A. impeachment	D. solicitous interest in
B. lionization	E. lack of involvement in
C. denouncement	F. malevolent attachment to

73. Joshua, a Jewish writer, who as a boy survived the holocausts in Nazi Germany, has a distinctively (i) _____ worldview: he sees through the (ii) _____ of good manners into the animal inside of even the common-man in human societies.

Blank (i)	Blank (ii)
A. cynical	D. veneer
B. utopian	E. pith
C. quixotic	F. panacea

74. Jerome earnestly (i) _____, after he had been found guilt of treason: he explained the circumstances under which the act had been performed, which seemed, at least so far as he was concerned, to (ii) _____ the deed.

Blank (i)	Blank (ii)
A. hollered for retribution	D. exacerbate
B. supplicated for forgiveness	E. extenuate
C. genuflected with acquiescence	F. formulate

75. Wagner became (i) _____ presence in Nietzsche's life, providing him with a model of philosophical sensibility that inspired him throughout his life. Like Wagner, Nietzsche was painfully responsive to the mutability of beauty and the (ii) _____ of youth, and therefore yearned for immortality through philosophy.

Blank (i)	Blank (ii)
A. an enduring	D. evanescence
B. a perfidious	E. caprice
C. a balking	F. rapture

76. In the event of a huge company failing to pay salaries to its employees, legal courses of action for such employees are (i) _____, yet the delay and expenses associate with these courses of action make it (ii) _____ to develop other options.

Blank (i)	Blank (ii)
A. accessible	D. imperative
B. unavailable	E. impractical
C. required	F. ridiculous

77. Modern astronomers find the views of pre-Galilean astronomers, regarding the history of the cosmos, (i) _____ and irrelevant. They therefore perceive these views as only of (ii) _____ interest.

Blank (i)	Blank (ii)
A. obsolete	D. historical
B. theoretical	E. seminal
C. sapient	F. sartorial

78. Although not the only (i) _____ of the new legislative reform, Ferguson was the (ii) _____, bringing into actualization the various aspects of the reform in the rural sector, which was the focal area of the reform.

Blank (i)	Blank (ii)
A. debaser	D. catalyst
B. proponent	E. filibuster
C. heckler	F. matron

79. The artistic collection of Harold Archie, an Irish street painter, exhibited in the contemporary arts gallery, has received (i) _____ (ii) _____ from critics: every single reviewer expressed his sense of amazement and marvel at his exhibits.

Blank (i)	Blank (ii)
A. reserved	D. approbation
B. unstinting	E. hostility
C. belligerent	F. criticism

80. According to Cesar Millan, a dog behavior expert, some dogs can be quite nervous and insecure by nature – but this can be (i) _____ when their master is calm and assertive; yet, when paired with a master who does not project calm and assertive confidence, the dog's insecurities might become (ii) _____.

Blank (i)	Blank (ii)
A. aggravated	D. inconsequential
B. settled	E. mollified
C. aggrandized	F. amplified

3-blanks TC questions

81. Undeniably, while men have a single, relatively simple and effective measure for contraception, women are afforded a _____ of alternatives that suit their lifestyles, predilections, and personal habits. However, for women's sake, this _____ of options should never be viewed as too varied or as _____.

Blank (i)	Blank (ii)	Blank (iii)
A. plethora	D. habiliment	G. repugnant
B. dearth	E. hodgepodge	H. deleterious
C. vestige	F. dearth	I. supernumerary

82. Aston was victim to several (i) _____ from his superiors, yet he put up a (ii) _____ countenance. Unfortunately, this very quality was viewed by many of his colleagues as (iii) _____ rather than as courage.

Blank (i)	Blank (ii)	Blank (iii)
A. approbations	D. composed	G. callousness
B. castigations	E. distressed	H. propriety
C. insubordinations	F. apathetic	I. competence

83. The new code of ethics is (i) _____; its guidelines are either (ii) _____, offering no perspectives but the obvious, or are so devoid of specific advice as to make almost any action (iii) _____.

Blank (i)	Blank (ii)	Blank (iii)
A. indubitable	D. platitudinous	G. unacceptable
B. laughable	E. homogeneous	H. justifiable
C. compendious	F. corroborative	I. impartial

84. Killer whales are (i) _____, familial animals, reliant on intense and (ii) _____ bonds for food, comfort, and fun. Their families and societies are (iii) _____: female whales live the longest and know the most, and their descendants live with them forever. Families live and hunt together in small groups called pods that hold anywhere from 20 to 50 whales, and each pod uses specific calls.

Blank (i)	Blank (ii)	Blank (iii)
A. gregarious	D. ephemeral	G. matriarchal
B. effeminate	E. enduring	H. anarchic
C. sanctimonious	F. unorthodox	I. unscrupulous

85. Being (i) _____ liar, Ronald had the power to make even the most far-fetched lies sound (ii) _____; yet, the fact that he could not make himself believable when telling the truth (iii) _____ him.

Blank (i)	Blank (ii)	Blank (iii)
A. a gauche	D. plausible	G. frustrated
B. a fallacious	E. grandiose	H. placated
C. an adroit	F. insincere	I. distraught

86. Hydrothermal vents, also called deep-sea vents, are (i) _____ by microbiologists, because in such small, controlled environments the enormously large assortment of microbial species complexity is (ii) _____ a scientifically (iii) _____ complexity.

Blank (i)	Blank (ii)	Blank (iii)
A. detested	D. relegated to	G. tractable
B. ignored	E. reduced to	H. diverse
C. prized	F. aggrandized with	I. intimidating

87. Though most ancient scrolls were (i) _____ preserved, enough have survived to allow us to (ii) _____ an occasionally interrupted but generally (iii) _____ progress of literary thought and philosophy.

Blank (i)	Blank (ii)	Blank (iii)
A. unwittingly	D. coruscate	G. documented
B. seldom	E. demonstrate	H. incessant
C. meticulously	F. controvert	I. noticeable

88. It is considered (i) _____, even a sign of madness when someone directly (ii) _____ a generally accepted system of values; but in the early renaissance period, such (iii) _____ behavior was idolized.

Blank (i)	Blank (ii)	Blank (iii)
A. frivolous	D. legislates	G. delusional
B. perspicacious	E. flouts	H. iconoclastic
C. sociopathic	F. acquiesces	I. conservative

89. When the prospect of starring in "The Martian" arose, Damon felt (i) _____: on the one hand, undertaking an adaptation of Andy Weir's bestselling novel, which blends hard science, humor and a suspenseful survival story, sounded (ii) _____, particularly with the electrified director, Scott, who'd made the sci-fi classics "Alien" and "Blade Runner," at the helm. On the other hand, the idea of immediately following "Interstellar," in which he played an astronaut stuck alone on an ice planet, with another role as a stranded astronaut had him (iii) _____.

Blank (i)	Blank (ii)	Blank (iii)
A. incensed	D. stimulating	G. give pause
B. ambivalent	E. laconic	H. dive in head first
C. determined	F. hackneyed	I. fired up

90. Worker bees are sterile females that supply the colony with food, acting as (i) _____, as the (ii) _____ queen produces enough (iii) _____ to continually populate the colony

Blank (i)	Blank (ii)	Blank (iii)
A. sentries	D. fecund	G. progeny
B. sages	E. captious	H. ancestors
C. laborers	F. abominable	I. harbingers

91. The mayor, in spite of the mounting criticism, (i) _____ the opposition. Not only has he (ii) _____ that revamping the health plan would be successful but also that it would achieve exactly what his proposal had (iii) _____ it would.

Blank (i)	Blank (ii)	Blank (iii)
A. refuted	D. insinuated	G. equivocated
B. vindicated	E. demonstrated	H. prognosticated
C. instigated	F. divagated	I. disabused

92. Despite projecting an image of (i) _____, most empires are actually (ii) _____ organism. A look at their history reminds us of how delicate their ecology of power is; when things start to go truly bad, these empires regularly (iii) _____with unholy speed.

Blank (i)	Blank (ii)	Blank (iii)
A. ineptitude	D. macroscopic	G. proliferate
B. omnipotence	E. insuperable	H. pullulate
C. animosity	F. fallible	I. unravel

93. The CEO of Cyber-con, an online computing service provider, (i) _____ the increasingly concerned investors by pointing out that despite its many (ii) _____, the newly developed cloud operating system that would make expensive hardware unnecessary, has gained (iii) _____ among startups and rapidly growing IT firms, who will make up the majority of their client base in the future.

Blank (i)	Blank (ii)	Blank (iii)
A. excoriated	D. proponents	G. disrepute
B. vilified	E. detractors	H. diminution
C. placated	F. exponents	I. currency

94. Being an (i) _____ makes it difficult to make the kind of (ii) _____ decisions that are alone considered a sign of competency in a (iii) _____ corporate environment.

Blank (i)	Blank (ii)	Blank (iii)
A. intellect	D. dysfunctional	G. pragmatic
B. idealist	E. evenhanded	H. esoteric
C. elitist	F. hardheaded	I. parsimonious

95. The court decided to (i) _____ the man who was responsible for the heinous crimes committed against several of Jefferson's family members; this led the next of kin, who were present at the court hearing, to (ii) _____ the judiciary system calling it a (iii) _____.

Blank (i)	Blank (ii)	Blank (iii)
A. exculpate	D. chastise	G. bastion
B. expurgate	E. rhapsodize	H. travesty
C. expatiate	F. lubricate	I. laggard

96. Synaesthesia, the production of a sense impression relating to one sense or part of the body by stimulation of another sense or part of the body, is generally categorized as a disability. Yet, occasionally it can be (i) _____: some people with synesthesia (ii) _____ sensory impulses in a way that allows them to interpret the world in a completely novel way, this inspires them into creating surreal works of art, which would have been (iii) _____ for a normal person to create.

Blank (i)	Blank (ii)	Blank (iii)
A. advantageous	D. cannot appreciate	G. inconceivable
B. intense	E. miss out on	H. indistinguishable
C. serious	F. can discern	I. appealing

97. Ironically, Emily's recent novel has been subject to much criticism for its (i) _____ structure, since, traditionally, critics have argued that her greatest (ii) _____ is that her works are (iii) _____ in their framework.

Blank (i)	Blank (ii)	Blank (iii)
A. attention to	D. shortcoming	G. relentlessly rigid
B. parody of	E. preoccupation	H. affably fatuous
C. lack of	F. characteristic	I. incomprehensibly cryptic

98. The drought of 1956 resulted in a substantial (i) _____ between crop supply and demand; as a consequence, this resulted in food product prices becoming so (ii) _____ that suppliers were generally thought to be (iii) _____ the customer.

Blank (i)	Blank (ii)	Blank (iii)
A. disparity	D. shielded	G. gouging
B. consanguinity	E. depressed	H. blackmailing
C. heterogeneity	F. prohibitive	I. placating

99. Although Rodrigues, the Spanish Director, was (i) _____ at (ii) _____ to appear innovative and spontaneous, beneath the (iii) _____ he remained uninspired and rigid in his approach to creating movies.

Blank (i)	Blank (ii)	Blank (iii)
A. abstemious	D. contriving	G. guise
B. ingenious	E. intending	H. impeccability
C. inept	F. deserving	I. contriteness

100. Augustine, a religious philosopher, believed in a benevolent god of (i) _____ whose nature was to create (ii) _____; he (iii) _____ his conception of an infinite universe from this 'infinite' God in whom he believed in.

Blank (i)	Blank (ii)	Blank (iii)
A. plentitude	D. temperance	G. arrogated
B. indulgence	E. dissension	H. separated
C. truculence	F. abundance	I. derived

Chapter 6

Sentence Equivalence – Solutions

1. Let us understand the meaning of the sentence from the partial information.

It states that Nepal's earthquake had *almost* devastated the capital city. With the use of signal word 'however', we can get the direction of the thought; it means that the following thought would be opposite of what is stated in the first part of the sentence. So NDRF team must have worked day and night to **lessen** the devastation.

So, we got our pre-empt **fill-in**; it should be a relatable word from the synonym family of **lessen**.

Let us understand the meanings of the option words.

(A) alleviate – to lessen or reduce; mitigate

(B) resuscitate – to restore to use, activity, vigor, or notice; reinvigorate

(C) mollify – appease the anger or anxiety of (someone)

(D) aggravate – worsen; exacerbate; intensify

(E) forestall – to prevent, hinder, or thwart by action in advance

(F) amputate – to prune, lop off, or remove

The correct answers would be 'alleviate' and 'forestall'. While 'aggravate' is the antonym of what we need, other words are not relevant for the **fill-in**. If you have a challenge in knowing the meaning of each word, you can at least infer the meaning of 'forestall'. When we break 'forestall' into syllables, we get 'fore + stall'; while 'fore' means 'before', 'stall' means 'to hold, to delay or put off'; thus, for the sentence 'forestall' serves the purpose well. However, we recommend learning vocabulary well.

The correct answers are A & E.

2. Let us understand the meaning of the sentence from the partial information.

It states that the Nash is a proud and aggressive mathematical genius who couldn't handle success; the more his prowess as a mathematician increased, the more **something** his personal life became. The phrase 'Nash couldn't handle success' necessitates that his fame must have a negative impact on his personal life.

Let us pre-empt the **fill-in**; it should be a relatable word from the synonym family of **chaotic**.

Let us understand the meanings of the option words.

(A) tempestuous – characterized by violent emotions or actions; tumultuous

(B) capricious – impulsive or unpredictable

(C) auspicious – favorable or propitious; fortunate

(D) spiritual – concerned with, or affecting the soul

(E) unruffled – not agitated emotionally; calm

(F) rustic – charmingly simple or unsophisticated

The correct answers would be 'tempestuous' and 'capricious'. While 'unruffled' is opposite of what we want, other options might qualify but they do not have a negative undertone, which is necessary in the sentence.

The correct answers are A & B.

3. Let us understand the meaning of the sentence from the partial information.

    The sentence states that even though the Southern Ocean is the most isolated body on the planet, it is not exempt from **something**. The phrase 'exempt from' means 'free from.' Plugging that phrase in that part of the sentence, our sentence reads that the Southern Ocean is not free from **something**. Although Southern Ocean is isolated (implying you'd expect it to be free from interference), Southern ocean is (in reality) not free from **garbage/rubbish** because of wind and ocean currents and thus debris is common on its waters. Ultimately our sentence means that the Southern Ocean has **something**. What does it have? The part of the sentence after the comma, viz., 'debris' is common on its waters and shores' provides the hint. Our **fill-in** should agree with the hint. We need **something** which says that the Southern Ocean has garbage in it. It is polluted.

    Let us pre-empt the **fill-in**; it should be a word related to 'pollution.' It should belong to the synonym family of **pollution**.

    Let us understand the meanings of the option words.

    (A) defilement – the process of making something dirty or impure

    (B) purification – the process of cleaning up something

    (C) composure – the state of feeling calm and in control

    (D) imperturbability – impassivity, steadiness, calmness

    (E) adumbration – outline or sketch

    (F) contamination – the process of making something unclean

    The correct answers are 'defilement' and 'contamination'. 'Imperturbability' and 'composure' don't agree with the hint that the Southern Ocean is full of debris. There is no connection between the ocean being calm and it being polluted. 'Purification' contradicts the information given in the sentence. 'Adumbration' is irrelevant.

    The correct answers are A & F.

4. Let us understand the meaning of the sentence from the partial information.

    The sentence talks about the conditions in the indoor environment which are related to the growth of fungi. These conditions are high relative humidity and warmth. There is nothing to indicate that these conditions hinder fungi growth. There is no opposite direction signal word. So we will take the sentence to mean that these conditions are suitable to the growth of fungi and look for our **fill-in** accordingly.

    Let us pre-empt the **fill-in**; it should be a word related to 'suitable.' It should belong to the synonym family of **suitable**.

    Let us understand the meaning of option words.

    (A) apposite – suitable

    (B) deleterious – harmful

(C)   pernicious – damaging

(D)   hostile – unfavorable

(E)   inimical – adverse

(F)   conducive – tending to promote or assist

The correct answers are 'apposite' and 'conducive.' 'Deleterious,' 'pernicious,' 'hostile' and 'inimical' belong to the antonym family of 'suitable'.

The correct answers are A & F.

5.   Let us understand the meaning of the sentence from the partial information. The sentence says that if one party does **something** to a bilateral treaty (bilateral treaty = a treaty involving two parties), then the other party too can terminate the treaty or suspend its operation. The word 'too' is a big **hint** here. This means that the first party has done **something** which the second party is merely repeating. Now, we know that the second party has terminated or suspended the treaty. This means that the first party suspended or terminated the treaty first. In simpler words, it broke the treaty first.

Let us pre-empt the **fill-in**; it should be a word related to 'break.' It should belong to the synonym family of **break.**

Let us understand the meanings of the option words.

(A)   breaches – to break or violate

(B)   vituperates – to rebuke or criticize harshly or angrily

(C)   honors – to respect

(D)   vitiates – to reduce the value or quality of, to corrupt morally

(E)   abrogates – to cancel, invalidate, nullify

(F)   denigrates – to criticize unfairly, disparage

The correct answers are 'breaches' and 'abrogates.' Though 'vituperates' and 'denigrates' are relevant in the context, these are not potent enough to convey the desired meaning. 'Honors' is in the antonym family of 'breaks' in this context. There seems to be a contrary relation between one party honoring the treating and the other one breaking it. 'Vitiates' is irrelevant too.

The correct answers are A & E.

6.   Let us understand the meaning of the sentence from the partial information.

The sentence says that the man was gruff (which means abrupt and kind of rough in manner) and **something else**. According to the woman, the reason for that was the man's past wounds which made it difficult for him to get close to people. This last bit is a big **hint** for our **fill-in**. We need a **fill-in** which agrees with the **hint** 'not getting too close to anyone else.'

Let us pre-empt the **fill-in**; it should be a word related to 'reserved.' It should belong to the synonym family of **reserved**.

Let us understand the meaning of option words.

(A)   standoffish – reserved, haughty

(B)   sedulous – marked by persistent effort, diligent

(C)   aloof – emotionally reserved or indifferent

(D)   partisan – a strong supporter of a party, cause or person

(E)   nubile – of marriageable age

(F)   erudite – having or showing great knowledge or learning

The correct answers are 'standoffish' and 'aloof.' 'Sedulous,' 'partisan' and 'nubile' are irrelevant. 'Erudite' is incorrect too as there is no obvious connection between having good knowledge and being reserved.

The correct answers are A & C.

7. Let us understand the meaning of the sentence from the partial information.

The sentence says that Josh's dreams were illogical and **something else**. The conjunction 'and' is a parallel **signal word**. Hence our **fill-in** should go along with 'illogical.' Also, the latter part of the passage tells us that Josh sometimes dreamed he was a cheeseburger being eaten by Robert. That is bizarre and a pretty puzzling dream.

Let us pre-empt the **fill-in**; it should be a word related to 'puzzling.' It should belong to the synonym family of **puzzling**.

Let us understand the meaning of option words.

(A)   insightful – having or showing deep understanding, perceptive

(B)   mysterious – difficult or impossible to understand, explain or identify

(C)   inscrutable – impossible to understand or interpret, impossible to scrutinize

(D)   acerbic – sharp and forthright

(E)   laconic – using very few words, brief, concise

(F)   vivid – producing powerful emotions, producing a clear picture in your mind

The correct answers are 'mysterious' and 'inscrutable'. 'Insightful' belongs to the antonym family of 'puzzling.' 'Laconic' is incorrect because there is no connection between a dream being brief and it being puzzling. Same logic applies to 'vivid.' 'Acerbic' is irrelevant.

The correct answers are B & C.

8. Let us understand the meaning of the sentence from the partial information.

The sentence contrasts 'I' the story teller who has the benefit of hindsight with 'I' the **something else**. The term 'while' is a contrasting **signal word** here which tells us that there are two opposing 'I's being compared here. While the first 'I' has benefit of hindsight (which means looking back on your past), the second 'I' is 'wet behind the ears.' The phrase 'wet behind the ears' means someone too young or inexperienced. It is usually used for beginners. It is our **hint** for our **fill-in**.

Let us pre-empt the **fill-in**; it should be a word related to 'beginner.' It should belong to the synonym family of **beginner**.

Let us understand the meaning of option words.

   (A) novice – a person new to a job, a beginner

   (B) dilettante – a person who cultivates an interest in an art without any real commitment, a dabbler

   (C) tyro – a beginner

   (D) professional – a person qualified in a profession

   (E) aesthete – a person who is appreciative of and sensitive to an art and beauty

   (F) anchorite – a religious recluse

The correct answers are 'novice' and 'tyro.' 'Dilettante' does not fit in this context. 'Professional' belongs to the antonym family of 'beginner.' 'aesthete' and 'Anchorite' are irrelevant.

The correct answers are A & C.

9. Let us understand the meaning of the sentence from the partial information.

    It describes Jain monks and states that they live a life of extreme simplicity and **something**. The only **hint-word** in the sentence is **austerity**. Therefore the word **simplicity** or **lack of luxury** can work as **fill-in**.

    Let us pre-empt the **fill-in**; it should be relatable a word that brings the context of **lack of luxury**.

    Let us understand the meanings of the option words.

   (A) renunciation – the act of renouncing; sacrificing or giving up

   (B) prodigality – spending money or using resources freely and recklessly; wastefully extravagant

   (C) consternation – anxiety or dismay

   (D) abnegation – the act of renouncing or rejecting something

   (E) profligacy – recklessly extravagant or wasteful in the use of resources

   (F) perturbation – anxiety; mental uneasiness

    The correct answers would be 'renunciation' and 'abnegation' since they both bring in the context of living without luxury. The words 'consternation' and 'perturbation' are not relevant to the context of the sentence. The words 'prodigality' and 'profligacy' are opposites of what the context requires.

    The correct answers are A & D.

10. Let us understand the meaning of the sentence from the partial information.

    It describes the observed economic scenario in the U.S. and states that this **something** has confused and perplexed economists. The phenomenon is though job openings are higher than ever, the number of people looking for jobs has been very low. The **hint-phrases** "**more job openings…yet, percentage of adult…job stands at a very low level**" and "**has bedeviled economists**" suggest that the phenomenon is puzzling. The word **puzzle** can work as the **fill-in**.

    Let us pre-empt the **fill-in**; it should be relatable a word that brings the context of **puzzle**.

    Let us understand the meanings of the option words.

(A) lampoon – public criticism by using ridicule, sarcasm or irony

(B) providence – timely preparation for future eventualities

(C) conundrum – confusing or difficult problem

(D) quandary – difficult situation; practical dilemma

(E) serendipity – occurrence and development of events by chance in a happy or beneficial way

(F) parody – imitation of the style of a particular writer, artist, or genre with deliberate exaggeration for comic effect

The correct answers would be 'conundrum' and 'quandary' since they both bring in the context of a 'difficult situation' or a 'puzzle'. The words 'lampoon' and 'parody' do not match the context of the sentence. The words 'providence' and 'serendipity' bring a positive undertone and do not bring in a context of something confusing or puzzling – they are therefore not relevant to what the sentence requires.

The correct answers are C & D.

11.   Let us understand the meaning of the sentence from the partial information.

It states that even if his ideas are **banal** (commonplace), due to his personality, people won't categorize his work in **some way**. Sentence provides us the **hint** for the **fill-in**. **Some way** is a characteristic that describes banal ideas. And with the use of signal word 'still', we can get the direction of the thought; it means that the following thought would be opposite of what is stated in the first part of the sentence. So **fill-in** must be **antonym of banal**.

So, we got our pre-empt **fill-in**; it should be a relatable word from the synonym family of **new**. Also, we should note that the **fill-in** has positive tone.

Let us understand the meanings of the option words.

(A) orthodox – following or conforming to the traditional or generally accepted rules or beliefs

(B) bizarre – unconventional; odd; unusual

(C) original – created personally by a particular artist

(D) paltry – not worth considering

(E) conventional – based on or in accordance with what is generally done or believed

(F) innovative – featuring new ideas

The correct answers would be 'original' and 'innovative'. While 'orthodox', 'paltry' and 'conventional' are opposite of hint word 'new', 'bizarre' can be looked as a good trap. 'Bizarre' means unconventional/odd; however it's worth noting that the sentence demands a positive **fill-in** word.

The correct answers are C & F.

12.   Let us understand the meaning of the sentence from the partial information.

It states that the fox has to be fall in the hole for which the hole is covered in a **particular manner** with finely sifted dirt.

Sentence provides us the **hint** for the **fill-in**. **Particular manner** is a characteristic that describes the idea of falling.

So, we got our pre-empt **fill-in**; it should be a relatable word from the synonym family of **loosely**.

Let us understand the meanings of the option words.

- **(A)** permanently – is the antonym of loosely

- **(B)** imperceptibly – so slight, gradual, or subtle as not to be perceived

- **(C)** sporadically – something that happens or appears often, but not constantly or regularly

- **(D)** precariously – characterized by a lack of security or stability

- **(E)** slightly – to a small degree; not considerably

- **(F)** unsteadily – not firm or solid

The correct answers would be 'precariously' and 'unsteadily'. While 'slightly' and 'sporadically' may be chosen by many students, it has to be considered that 'slightly' means that it is covered to a small degree which may lead to the event in which the fox does not walk over and 'sporadically' means not constant which does not guarantee the fox's fall. 'Imperceptibly' means not to be perceived. This may give us the sense that the fox will walk over it. However the sentence demands the fox to not only walk over but also fall in the hole. Hence, we can't use it in the sentence as the provided hint is not referring to this.

The correct answers are D & F.

13. Let us understand the meaning of the sentence from the partial information.

It states that the project was completed in **certain way,** and team members worked together. The signal word **but** contrast the **fill-in**. While 'unintelligently' describes 'the team did not optimize the limited resources', **Certain way** must describe 'team's working closely together'. Thus, the sentence provides us the **hint** for the **fill-in**.

So, we got our pre-empt **fill-in**; it should be a relatable word from the synonym family of **together**.

Let us understand the meanings of the option words.

- **(A)** competitively – involving competition
- **(B)** passionately – having powerful emotions
- **(C)** cooperatively – working or acting together
- **(D)** deviously – tending to lie and tricking
- **(E)** craftily – cleverly
- **(F)** amicably – friendly or with goodwill

The correct answers would be 'cooperatively' and 'amicably'. While 'deviously', 'craftily' and 'competitively' are relatable words from the antonym family of **hint word** 'together', 'passionately' can be looked as a trap. 'Passionately' means having powerful emotions, however given the limited information, we cannot infer that the project was necessarily completed with an emotional touch but with togetherness. Since only two options are correct, thus while considering 'cooperatively' and 'amicably', 'passionately' cannot be the correct option.

The correct answers are C and F.

14. Let us understand the meaning of the sentence from the partial information.

The sentence begins with the signal word 'although'. This clearly tells us that the direction of the sentence in the later part would change. The sentence states that students showed **certain behavior** during presentation, but the presenter did her best to involve them in active conversation. Sentence provides us the **hint** for the **fill-in Certain behavior** is a characteristic that describes opposite of **active conversation.**

So, we got our pre-empt **fill-in**; it should be a relatable word from the synonym family of **inactive.**

Let us understand the meanings of the option words.

(A) loquacious – talkative

(B) taciturn – reserved

(C) arbitrary – based on random choice

(D) reticent – reserved

(E) tractable – easy to control

(F) garrulous – excessively talkative

The correct answers would be 'taciturn' and 'reticent'. While 'loquacious' and 'garrulous' are opposite of **hint 'inactive'**, 'arbitrary' and 'tractable' can be easily eliminated as neither the 'random choice' nor 'control' is implied in the sentence.

The correct answers are B and D.

15. Let us understand the meaning of the sentence from the partial information.

It states that Jeremy Campbell portrays an image of having achieved holistic congruity by doing **something** with contradictory elements of his life. The **hint** for what the 'something' is lies in the word **holistic congruity**. Based on the **hint** it is apparent that he must have **made peace with** the contradictory elements to achieve holistic congruity.

Let us pre-empt the **fill-in**; it should be a relatable word from the synonym family of **made peace with.**

Let us understand the meanings of the option words.

(A) plagiarized – taken someone else's idea or work and pass it off as your own

(B) ostracized – excluded or banished from a society or group

(C) reconciled – settled a conflict or disagreement

(D) confined – restricted in area or volume

(E) resolved – settled or found a solution to a problem or a conflict

(F) vilified – spoke or wrote about in an abusively disparaging manner

The correct answers are 'reconciled' and 'resolved'. 'Plagiarized', 'ostracized' and 'vilified' do not make sense in context as they do not convey the meaning of 'made peace with'. 'Confined' has a negative connotation in this context and is therefore not a good **fill-in**.

The correct answers are C & E.

16. Let us understand the meaning of the sentence from the partial information.

It states what the technology expert feels about the journal. With the use of signal word '**not**', we can get the direction of the thought; it means that the following thought would be opposite of what is stated about the expert's expectation from the **world's greatest publisher**.

So, we got our pre-empt **fill-in**; it should be something opposite to 'professional' and therefore, could be words which are relatable to the synonym family of **non-professional**.

Let us understand the meanings of the option words.

(A) luddite – a person who is against technology and industrialization

(B) dilettante – a person who cultivates an area of interest, such as the arts, without real commitment or knowledge.

(C) virtuoso – a person highly skilled in music or another artistic pursuit

(D) veteran – a person who has had long experience in a particular field

(E) sciolist – a person who pretends to be knowledgeable and well informed

(F) itinerant – a person who travels from place to place

The correct answers would be 'dilettante and 'sciolist'. While 'virtuoso' and 'veteran' are the antonyms of what we need, other words are not relevant for the **fill-in**.

The correct answers are B & E.

17. Let us understand the meaning of the sentence from the partial information.

It states that Lady Gaga was, in her private life, **some kind** of person. The sentence provides the **hint-word** for the **fill-in** in the first part of the sentence. We know that her artistic works were **flamboyant** and that her private life was in contrast to this. We know this because of the word **surprisingly**, which is a contrasting signal word.

Let us pre-empt the **fill-in**; it should be a relatable word from the synonym family of **down to earth**.

Let us understand the meanings of the option words.

(A) unostentatious – not pretentious; simple or plain

(B) audacious – showing impudent lack of respect; surprisingly bold

(C) simple – plain, basic or uncomplicated

(D) unorthodox – contrary to what is usual; unconventional

(E) imprudent – not showing care for the consequence of an action; rash

(F) controversial – giving rise to public disagreement

The correct answers would be 'unostentatious' and 'simple'. 'Unorthodox' and 'controversial' are opposite of what we want. 'Audacious' and 'imprudent' have a negative undertone, which does not fit the context.

The correct answers are A & C.

18. Let us understand the meaning of the sentence from the partial information.

It states that Jacques's new short-film is likely to appeal an international audience. The **hint** provided in the sentence about the short-film is that it is dissimilar to other short-movies, which have **strictly regional themes**. The use of the signal word **not** suggests that Jacques's movies are not **local**.

Let us pre-empt the **fill-in**; it should be a relatable word from the synonym family of **local**.

Let us understand the meanings of the option words.

   (A) complex – not easy to understand

   (B) domestic – existing or occurring inside a particular region; not international

   (C) populist – supporting concerns of ordinary people

   (D) provincial – concerning a particular region or country

   (E) democratic – favoring social equality

   (F) byzantine – excessively complicated

The correct answers would be 'domestic' and 'provincial'. The words 'populist', 'democratic' 'complex' and 'byzantine' do not fit the required context.

The correct answers are B & D.

19. Let us understand the meaning of the sentence from the partial information.

It states that the senator was **doing something** against the city bureaucracy. The later part of the sentence mentions the senator described the bureaucracy as **"bumbling and bungling"**; these serve as our **hint-words**. Considering the **hint-words**, we realize that what he did was to point out the flaws in the bureaucracy; therefore, the word **"complaining** against" will fit the context of the sentence and serve as the **fill-in**.

Let us pre-empt the **fill-in**; it should be a relatable word from the synonym family of **complaining**.

Let us understand the meanings of the option words.

   (A) railing – complaining or protesting strongly about something

   (B) corroborating – giving conformation to or supporting something

   (C) edifying – providing moral or intellectual instruction

   (D) inveighing – speaking or writing about something with great hostility

   (E) indoctrinating – teaching someone to accept a set of beliefs uncritically

   (F) endorsing – declaring one's public approval or support for something

The correct answers would be 'railing' and 'inveighing'. 'Corroborating' and 'endorsing' are opposites of what is required. 'Edifying' and 'indoctrinating' do not fit the context of the sentence.

The correct answers are A & D.

20. Let us understand the meaning of the sentence from the partial information.

It states that a particular concept is so simple to state and understand that the there is a tendency to **do something** with respect to its significance. The **hint-word** here is **so simple**, suggesting that this concept could be taken for granted or undervalued. A good **fill-in** based on the context is "**underestimate.**"

Let us pre-empt the **fill-in**; it should be a relatable word from the synonym family of **underestimate**.

Let us understand the meanings of the option words.

   (A) approbate – approve formally; sanction

   (B) articulate – pronounce clearly and distinctively

   (C) trivialize – make something seem less important than what it actually is

   (D) enunciate – say or pronounce clearly

   (E) praise – express warm approval or admiration

   (F) underrate – underestimate the importance of something

The correct answers would be 'trivialize' and 'underrate'. The words 'approbate' and 'praise' are opposite of what the sentence requires. 'Articulate' and 'enunciate' do not fit the required context.

The correct answers are C & F.

21. Let us understand the meaning of the sentence from the partial information.

It states that people who enter Hollywood often swap the **some kind of** names they are given by their parents with more interesting or fancy ones. The **hint-words** here are **swap** and **exotic** and this provides sufficient information to predict the **fill-in**. Based on the **hint-words** we realize that the names they were born with were **ordinary**.

Let us pre-empt the **fill-in**; it should be a relatable word from the synonym family of **ordinary**.

Let us understand the meanings of the option words.

   (A) scintillating – sparking or shining brightly

   (B) ambiguous – doubtful or uncertain

   (C) pedestrian – lacking inspiration or excitement; dull

   (D) evocative – bringing strong images, memories, or feelings to mind

   (E) quotidian – ordinary or everyday; mundane

   (F) dubious – morally suspect; having questionable value

The correct answers would be 'pedestrian' and 'quotidian'. The words 'scintillating' and 'evocative' are positive adjectives and thus are opposite of what we need. Though 'dubious' and 'ambiguous' are negative in meaning; they do not suit the context.

The correct answers are C & E.

22. Let us understand the meaning of the sentence from the partial information.

It states that the father adores his child and that he cannot be accused of **doing something** with his affection for her. The **hint-word** in the sentence is that his conduct betrays his **immense love** for her. The word **cannot** present in the sentence acts as the **signal word**. This gives us an idea of what the **fill-in** must be: we realize that he cannot be accused of **holding back** his affection for his daughter.

Let us pre-empt the **fill-in**; it should be a relatable word from the synonym family of **holding back**.

Let us understand the meanings of the option words.

(A) lavishing – giving in generous amounts to someone

(B) stinting – restricting the amount given to someone

(C) limiting – restricting the amount of something

(D) indulging – allowing someone to enjoy something desired

(E) propagandizing – promoting a particular view or cause

(F) touting – attempting to persuade people of the merit of something

The correct answers would be 'stinting' and 'limiting'. The words 'lavishing' and 'indulging' are opposite of what the sentence requires. 'Propagandizing' and 'touting' do not fit the required context.

The correct answers are B & C.

23. Let us understand the meaning of the sentence from the partial information.

It states that the contestant was the judge's friend and this opened the judge to accusations that he lacked **something**. The **hint-word** can be found in the latter part of the sentence and it conveys the meaning that the judge did not have **bias**. The use of '**did not necessarily imply**' acts as a **signal phrase** suggesting that the judge was probably **impartiality**.

Let us pre-empt the **fill-in**; it should be a relatable word from the synonym family of **impartiality**.

Let us understand the meanings of the option words.

(A) composure – state of being calm and in control of oneself

(B) disinterestedness – state of being uninfluenced by considerations of personal advantage; being impartial

(C) disparateness – state of being so different as to have no basis for comparison

(D) impassiveness – state of not feeling or showing emotion

(E) dispassionateness – state of being uninfluenced by emotion; state of being impartial

(F)   clairvoyance –ability to see into the future

The correct answers would be 'disinterestedness' and 'dispassionateness'. The words 'composure', disparateness' and 'clairvoyance' do not fit the context of the sentence. 'Impassiveness' has a negative undertone; it means to be lack emotion and but it does not fit the context of partiality.

The correct answers are B & E.

24.   Let us understand the meaning of the sentence from the partial information.

It states that David acted in a way that suggested that he was deeply interested in his employee's work, but in actuality he only had a **some kind** of interest. The phrase '**almost non-existent**' serves as the **hint-phrase**. 'Although' at the beginning of the sentence acts as a **signal word** and suggests that the way he acted did not reflect his true feelings. Based on the hints provided, the word **shallow** will serve as an appropriate **fill-in**.

Let us pre-empt the **fill-in**; it should be a relatable word from the synonym family of **shallow**.

Let us understand the meanings of the option words.

(A)   perfunctory – without much interest or feeling

(B)   profound – very large or intense

(C)   superficial – existing on a surface level; shallow

(D)   preemptive – serving to prevent or forestall something

(E)   imperative – vitally important; crucial

(F)   ardent – very enthusiastic or passionate

The correct answers would be 'perfunctory' and 'superficial'. The words 'profound' and 'ardent' are opposites of what the sentence requires. The words 'preemptive' and 'imperative' do not fit the context of the sentence.

The correct answers are A & C.

25.   Let us understand the meaning of the sentence from the partial information.

It states that he is very careful with money and that this quality should not be confused for his **being something**. The **signal phrase** here is **should not be confused with**. The phrase **willing to assist** serves as the **hint-phrase** for the sentence. Based on these hints it becomes clear that his thriftiness should not be confused with **stinginess**.

Let us pre-empt the **fill-in**; it should be a relatable word from the synonym family of **stinginess**.

Let us understand the meanings of the option words.

(A)   impecuniousness – a state of being very poor with little or no money

(B)   parsimoniousness – a state of being very unwilling to spend money

(C)   indigence – a state of extreme poverty

(D)   exuberance – the quality of being full of energy

(E)   niggardliness – a state of being extremely stingy with money

(F) perspicacity – the quality of having a ready insight into things

The correct answers would be 'parsimoniousness' and 'niggardliness'. The words 'impecuniousness' and 'indigence' suggest being extremely poor and not necessarily of being stingy; they are, therefore, not relevant to the context. The words 'exuberance' and 'perspicacity' are not relevant to the context of the sentence.

The correct answers are B & E.

26. Let us understand the meaning of the sentence from the partial information.

It states that though nature acts aggressively against lethal hereditary diseases they are not as **something** as expected. The phrase "**eliminates genetic materials**" acts as the **hint-phrase**. The word **paradoxically** is a **signal word** and conveys the meaning that these hereditary diseases do not follow the logic implied in the first part of the sentence. The idea is that although these lethal diseases must be 'not so common', they are paradoxically 'common'. The word '**not**' acts as the **second signal word**: the **fill-in** here will be '**not so common**'.

Let us pre-empt the **fill-in**; it should be relatable adjectives from the synonym family of **not so common**.

Let us understand the meanings of the option words.

(A) pervasive – spreading widely throughout an area

(B) infrequent – not occurring very often

(C) ubiquitous – present everywhere

(D) daunting – causing fear or discouragement; intimidating

(E) scarce – occurring in small numbers or quantities; rare

(F) appalling – causing horror; frightful

The correct answers would be 'infrequent' and 'scarce'. The words 'pervasive' and 'ubiquitous' are opposite of what is required. The words 'daunting' and 'appalling' do not fit the context of the sentence.

The correct answers are B & E.

27. Let us understand the meaning of the sentence from the partial information.

It states that through comedy, topics that are considered **something** over dinner conversations or even on television can be brought into discussion. The **hint-phrase** here is that these are topics that **would otherwise be avoided**. Another clue is the word **facetiousness**, which implies that comedy makes light of serious matters. This suggests that the **fill-in** must be a word that has the quality of being serious; it must also have a negative undertone since the sentence states that such topics must be "avoided". "**Off limits**" works well in context.

Let us pre-empt the **fill-in**; it should be a relatable word from the synonym family of **off limits**.

Let us understand the meanings of the option words.

(A) approbation – approval or praise

(B)   pontification – self-important expression of opinion or prejudice

(C)   anathema – something that is greatly disliked or viewed with disgust

(D)   defenestration – the act of throwing someone or something out of the window

(E)   taboo – something that is prohibited or restricted by social custom

(F)   placation – the act of lowering the anger or hostility of someone or something

The correct answers would be 'anathema' and 'taboo'. 'Approbation' and 'placation' are opposite to what the sentence requires. ' Pontification' and 'defenestration' are not relevant to the context of the sentence.

The correct answers are C & E.

28.   Let us understand the meaning of the sentence from the partial information.

It states what the management theory postulates that it is desirable to increase employee productivity if **some kinds** of increases are also not necessary in aspects that involve the company's contribution to the employee's development. The clues here are more contextual than direct. The context suggests that the employee must be expected to be more productive if the company has invested money and time on him or her. Therefore, the word **comparable** can act as the **fill-in**.

Let us pre-empt the **fill-in**; it should be a relatable word from the synonym family of **comparable**.

Let us understand the meanings of the option words.

(A)   commensurate – corresponding in size or degree; proportionate

(B)   asymmetrical – unequal in parts or distribution

(C)   zealous – extremely passionate and energetic towards something

(D)   proportionate – corresponding in size or amount

(E)   amorphous – lacking a clear structure or focus

(F)   jingoistic – extremely patriotic

The correct answers would be 'commensurate' and 'proportionate'. The words 'asymmetrical' is opposite to what the sentence requires. The words 'zealous', 'amorphous' and 'jingoistic' are not relevant to the context of the sentence.

The correct answers are A & D.

29.   Let us understand the meaning of the sentence from the partial information.

It states that some of the information provided by the author about the Mayan civilization seems bizarre, but the major themes are **someway**. The contrasting signal word here is **though**; this interplays with the hint-word **bizarre**. Based on the clues, the word **normal** will act as the **fill-in**.

Let us pre-empt the **fill-in**; it should be a relatable word from the synonym family of **normal**.

Let us understand the meanings of the option words.

(A)   cryptic –mysterious or obscure

(B) hackneyed – overused and ordinary; unoriginal

(C) soporific – sleep inducing

(D) bromidic – ordinary; commonplace through overuse

(E) eccentric – unconventional and slightly strange

(F) grave – serious or solemn in manner or appearance

The correct answers would be 'hackneyed' and 'bromidic'. The words 'cryptic', and 'eccentric' are opposites of what the sentence requires. 'Soporific' and 'grave' do not fit the context of the sentence.

The correct answers are B & D.

30. Let us understand the meaning of the sentence from the partial information.

It states that Delta Ware followed a **certain way** after the corporate takeover. The latter part of the sentence '**flexible work culture replaced with bureaucracy and rigid policies**' acts as the **hint-phrase**. The word **inflexible** therefore fits the context.

Let us pre-empt the **fill-in**; it should be a relatable word from the synonym family of **inflexible**.

Let us understand the meanings of the option words.

(A) fossilized – incapable of change

(B) factious – inclined to disagreement or discord

(C) ungovernable – impossible to control

(D) ossified – set in rigidly conventional pattern; inflexible

(E) schismatic – something that promotes separation or division

(F) politicized – engaged in or talk about politics

The correct answers would be 'fossilized' and 'ossified'. The words 'schismatic' and 'factious' in context bring out a negative effect that might be plausible after a corporate takeover, but the clues in the sentence only suggest that the company became 'inflexible'; these two words do not mean 'inflexible' and can therefore be eliminated. The words 'ungovernable' and 'politicized' do not fit the context of the sentence.

The correct answers are A & D.

31. Let us understand the meaning of the sentence from the partial information.

It states that his parents were considered **something** because they refused to follow a specific law that they were meant to follow at that time. The phrasal contraction "**refused to attend…as required by law**" acts as the **hint-phrase**. The word **rebels** can therefore work as the **fill-in**.

Let us pre-empt the **fill-in**; it should be a relatable word from the synonym family of **rebels**.

Let us understand the meanings of the option words.

(A) proletariats – people of the working-class

(B) patriarchs – male heads of a family or tribe

(C) conservatives – people who are reluctant to accept changes and new ideas

(D) recusants – people who refuse to conform to established standards

(E) conformists – people who strictly follow established customs or doctrines

(F) heretics – people who go against established standards and beliefs

The correct answers would be 'recusants' and 'heretics'. The words 'conservatives' and 'conformists' are opposite to what the sentence requires. The words 'proletariats' and 'patriarchs' are not relevant to the context of the sentence.

The correct answers are D & F.

32. Let us understand the meaning of the sentence from the partial information.

It states that although good relationships are not easy, they nurture love even when you have **a certain characteristic** or are petulant (irritable). The **hint-word** here is **petulant**, which is negative, thus the **fill-in** must also be a negative trait. Any negative human trait will act as the **fill-in**.

We cannot pre-empt the **fill-in** in this question; all we can infer is that the fill-in must be word, belonging to a negative human trait.

Let us understand the meanings of the option words.

(A) cantankerous – bad tempered and uncooperative

(B) staunch – believing something very strongly

(C) distended – swollen due to pressure from the inside; bloated

(D) committed – dedicated; bound to a certain course or policy

(E) curmudgeonly – ill-mannered and ill-tempered

(F) credulous – believing anything readily

The correct answers would be 'cantankerous' and 'curmudgeonly'. The words 'staunch', 'distended', 'committed' and 'credulous' do not either have negative traits or fit the context of the sentence.

The correct answers are A & E.

33. Let us understand the meaning of the sentence from the partial information.

It states that the senator **expresses in someway** his feelings to the opposition about the proposed policies. The latter part of the sentence provides the **hint-phrase** about the senator's opinion: he feels that the policies are **absurd and would have potentially devastating consequences**. Based on the clues, the word **criticized** can act as the **fill-in**.

Let us pre-empt the **fill-in**; it should be a relatable word from the synonym family of **criticized**.

Let us understand the meanings of the option words.

(A) persuaded – caused (someone) to accept a point of view by means of argument or reasoning

(B) castigated – scolded someone severely

(C) extolled – praised highly

(D)   excoriated – criticize someone severely

(E)   eulogized – praised highly in speech or writing

(F)   cajoled – persuaded someone through flattery

The correct answers would be 'castigated' and 'excoriated'. The words 'extolled' and 'eulogized' are opposites of what the sentence requires. The words 'persuaded' and 'cajoled' do not fit the context of the sentence.

The correct answers are B & D.

34.   Let us understand the meaning of the sentence from the partial information.

It describes that Johanne remains **someone** since in the past he was both a champion of democratization and a dictator who went against the principles of democracy. The **hint-phrase** can be found in the latter part of the sentence "**both a proponent of democratic change…and a harsh military dictator…**": this suggests that he has been known to act in a manner that is quite strange, mysterious or even self-contradictory. The **fill-in** could therefore be **a mystery**.

Let us pre-empt the **fill-in**; it should be a relatable word from the synonym family of **a mystery**.

Let us understand the meanings of the option words.

(A)   an enigma – a thing or a person that is mysterious or difficult to understand

(B)   a tyro – a person who is a beginner; a novice

(C)   a paradox – a person or thing that combines contradictory qualities

(D)   an anachronism – a thing or a person that is not appropriate to the time period it belongs in

(E)   a paragon – a person or thing that is regarded as the perfect example of a particular quality

(F)   a pedant – a person who is overly concerned with minor details and rules

The correct answers would be 'an enigma' and 'a paradox'. 'A tyro, 'an anachronism', 'a paragon' and 'a pedant' are not relevant to the context of the sentence.

The correct answers are A & C.

35.   Let us understand the meaning of the sentence from the partial information.

It states that the jury faced great difficulty to bring out general agreement (consensus) because its members had such **some type** of opinions. The **hint-phrase** is present in the initial part of the sentence, which says that the jury **had great difficulty forming a consensus**. This suggests that the members of the jury had very different or contrasting opinions. The **fill-in** can therefore be the adjective **contrasting**.

Let us pre-empt the **fill-in**; it should be a relatable word from the synonym family of **contrasting**.

Let us understand the meanings of the option words.

(A)   divergent – different from others

(B)   congruous – appropriate or harmonious

(C) jovial – joyous and good spirited

(D) disparate – fundamentally distinct or different in kind; entirely different

(E) flippant – disrespectful; lack of seriousness

(F) amicable – friendly and good willed

The correct answers would be 'divergent' and 'disparate'. The words 'congruous' is opposite to what the sentence requires. 'Jovial', 'flippant' and 'amicable' are not relevant to the context of the sentence.

The correct answers are A & D.

36. Let us understand the meaning of the sentence from the partial information.

It states that MacGill feels that the photograph is the most beautiful because of the subtleties it captures, yet to someone who cannot see or understand the subtleties the same photograph may look quite **a particular**. The **hint-phrase** is present in the first part of the sentence— MacGill feels that the photograph is the **most** beautiful he has ever seen. This is followed with the signal word '**yet**'. We, therefore, need a word that is opposite to '**most beautiful**'. The word **ordinary** will be the **fill-in**.

Let us pre-empt the **fill-in**; it should be a relatable word from the synonym family of **ordinary**.

Let us understand the meanings of the option words.

(A) pedestrian – dull; lacking in inspiration or excitement

(B) prosaic – lacking in imagination or spirit; dull

(C) despondent – low in spirit from loss of hope or courage; hopeless

(D) exuberant – full of enthusiasm or joy

(E) dogmatic – narrow minded or opinionated

(F) doleful – full of grief; mournful

The correct answers would be 'pedestrian' and 'prosaic'. The words 'exuberant' and 'dogmatic' are not relevant to the context of the sentence. The words 'despondent' and 'doleful' might seem like good fits, but a closer look at their meanings show that they both mean to be sad; the sentence does not bring in the context of 'sad' anywhere; the words 'despondent' and 'doleful' therefore do not match the context of the sentence.

The correct answers are A & B.

37. Let us understand the meaning of the sentence from the partial information.

It states that people have become "speed readers" and are focused more on reading in a **particular way** rather than reading by devoting a lot of time, effort and involvement. The **hint-phrase** here is **painstaking and absorbed**. The word **rather** than acts as the signal word. It suggests that people have become focused on reading that is shallow or on the **surface level**: this can be the **fill-in**.

Let us pre-empt the **fill-in**; it should be a relatable word from the synonym family of **surface level**.

Let us understand the meanings of the option words.

(A) pedantic – overly concerned with even small details

(B) exacting – careful and involving a lot of effort or attention

(C) lingering – continuing in a place or slow in leaving it

(D) cursory – performed very quickly without attention to detail

(E) fastidious – very careful and giving a lot of attention to detail

(F) perfunctory – done quickly without paying attention to detail; not thorough

The correct answers would be 'cursory' and 'perfunctory'. The word 'lingering' brings the meaning of persisting at a place for a long time; this is in some ways contrary to what the sentence requires. The words 'pedantic', 'exacting' and 'fastidious' when used in the sentence are opposites of the idea of 'surface level' and therefore do not match the context of the sentence.

The correct answers are D & F.

38. Let us understand the meaning of the sentence from the partial information.

It describes Wordsworth's poems as **something** because most of them may seem too sad or depressing to some people. The only clue here is the word **melancholic,** which is the **hint-word**. We need a word that means sad or depressing. The word **sorrowful** can be the **fill-in**.

Let us pre-empt the **fill-in**; it should be a relatable word from the synonym family of **sorrowful**.

Let us understand the meanings of the option words.

(A) hackneyed – repeated too often; overfamiliar through overuse

(B) pious – showing or expressing religious devotion

(C) bromidic – dull; ordinary

(D) doleful – expressing grief; mournful

(E) sanctimonious – showing false piety or righteousness

(F) plaintive – expressing sorrow; mournful

The correct answers are 'doleful' and 'plaintive'. The words 'hackneyed', and 'sanctimonious' are not relevant to the context of the sentence. 'Bromidic' is tricky one, but it is not the correct answer; it means dull and ordinary, whereas contextually, **fill-in** implies too sad or depressing, and not necessarily dull.

Although 'pious' might seem like a good fit, the word brings in a context of religious devotion and is not relevant to the content of the sentence, which is 'sorrowful' or 'sad'.

The correct answers are D & F.

39. Let us understand the meaning of the sentence from the partial information.

It states that the group expresses its opinion about 'cuts in the military budget' very openly, yet when it has to express its opinion about 'taxes' it turns to **doing something else**. The **hint-phrase** in the sentence is that the group is **plainly advocating** cuts in military budget. The signal word **while** suggests a contrast in the group's actions when talking taxes. A word that means opposite of openness or '**indirectness**' will act as the **fill-in**.

Let us pre-empt the **fill-in**; it should be a relatable word from the synonym family of **indirectness**.

Let us understand the meanings of the option words.

(A)   vituperation – verbal abuse or harsh criticism

(B)   cogency – persuasiveness by appealing to the intellect

(C)   circumlocution – roundabout or indirect way of speaking

(D)   interrogation – formal systematic questioning

(E)   euphemism – use of mild, indirect or vague term instead of the one that is considered harsh, blunt or offensive.

(F)   eloquence – use of powerful and effective language

The correct answers are 'circumlocution' and 'euphemism'. Although 'euphemism' brings the context of replacing a harsh word with a softer one, people use 'euphemisms' to be 'evasive' or 'indirect' while discussing a sensitive topic (in this case the 'taxes'); 'euphemism' therefore is within the scope of the sentence's context. The words 'vituperation', 'cogency', 'interrogation' and 'eloquence' do not fit the context of the sentence.

The correct answers are C & E.

40.   Let us understand the meaning of the sentence from the partial information.

It states that the result brings to mind an image of something done in an overly careful, controlling and industrious fashion where young minds are molded in a **certain way**. The words "**compartmentalized, overanalyzed, possibly totalitarian environment**", act as the **hint-words**. The word **intensely** can act as the **fill-in**.

Let us pre-empt the **fill-in**; it should be a relatable word from the synonym family of **intensely**.

Let us understand the meanings of the option words.

(A)   assiduously – very carefully and persistently

(B)   seductively – temptingly; enticingly

(C)   unstintingly – very generously

(D)   sedulously – constantly and persistently; assiduously

(E)   tantalizingly – attractively and temptingly

(F)   fatuously – foolishly or in a silly fashion

The correct answers are 'assiduously' and 'sedulously'. Though the words do not carry a negative undertone (and the sentence does), they are the only options that are closest to what the sentence requires in the context of 'intensely'. 'Seductively', 'tantalizingly' and 'fatuously' do not fit the context of the sentence. The word 'unstintingly' carries a positive undertone in the context of being generous, which does not match the required context of the sentence.

The correct answers are A & D.

41. Let us understand the meaning of the sentence from the partial information.

It describes the public's perspectives about Rushdie's work and states that it paradoxically drew both public support and **something else**. The **hint-word** here is **support**. The presence of the signal-word '**paradoxically**' suggests that the public had simultaneously contradictory perspectives about his work. The **fill-in** here needs to be contextually opposite to the word **support**; the word **objection** can therefore work here.

Let us pre-empt the **fill-in**; it should be a relatable word from the synonym family of **objection**.

Let us understand the meanings of the option words.

(A) denunciation – public condemnation

(B) impersonation – imitation; the act of deceiving

(C) reprobation – disapproval, blame or censure

(D) commendation – formal or official praise

(E) adulation – excessive admiration or praise

(F) imitation – to mimic something or someone; copy of an original

The correct answers would be 'denunciation' and 'reprobation'. The words 'impersonation' and 'imitation' are not relevant to the context of the sentence. The words 'commendation' and 'adulation' are in contrast to what the sentence requires and therefore do not match the context of the sentence.

The correct answers are A & C.

42. Let us understand the meaning of the sentence from the partial information.

It states that the trend of Industrial moguls entering politics has raised concerns that we may be close to creating **a type of government** in this country. The **hint-phrase** here about the type of government can be found in the latter part of the sentence: "**decisions made solely by a handful or very wealthy individuals**." The **fill-in** must therefore be relevant to either "**a type of government ruled by a small group**" or "**a type of government ruled by the wealthy**".

Let us pre-empt the **fill-in**; it should be a relatable word from the synonym family of either "**a type of government ruled by a small group**" or "**a type of government ruled by the wealthy**".

Let us understand the meanings of the option words.

(A) an oligarchy – a state governed by a few people

(B) an autocracy – a state that is governed by a single person with unlimited power

(C) a bureaucracy – a state governed by a rigid hierarchy of bureaus, administrators, and petty officials

(D) an adhocracy – an organization with little or no structure

(E) a plutocracy – a state in which the wealthy rule

(F) a theocracy – a state governed by religious authority

The correct answers would be 'an oligarchy' and 'a plutocracy'. 'An autocracy', 'a bureaucracy', 'an adhocracy' and 'a theocracy' do not fit the context of the sentence.

The correct answers are A & E.

43. Let us understand the meaning of the sentence from the partial information.

It states that Zuckerberg was considered **something** by his subordinates. The **hint-phrase** here is **'expected his every whim to be obeyed without question'**. We therefore need a negative word that captures this bossy or arrogant quality. The **fill-in** here will be **bossy**.

Let us pre-empt the **fill-in**; it should be a relatable word from the synonym family of **bossy**.

Let us understand the meanings of the option words.

(A) overbearing – domineering in manner; arrogant

(B) lubricious – lewd, lascivious

(C) insolent – offensive, impudent, or disrespectful

(D) flippant – disrespectful lack of seriousness

(E) imperious – arrogantly domineering or overbearing

(F) foolhardy – unwisely bold; rash

The correct answers would be 'overbearing' and 'imperious'. The words 'insolent' is very close but it does not carry the context of being bossy, it merely means to be disrespectful. The words 'lubricious', 'flippant' and 'foolhardy' are not relevant in context.

The correct answers are A & E.

44. Let us understand the meaning of the sentence from the partial information.

It states that writers, activists and consumers gave their opinion about Comcast, and gave it **a certain** title. The **hint-phrase** here is the title itself: "**worst company in America**". This suggests that the title was of a nature intended to defame or abuse. The word **abusive** can be used as the **fill-in**.

Let us pre-empt the **fill-in**; it should be a relatable word from the synonym family of.

Let us understand the meanings of the option words.

(A) mundane – commonplace; ordinary

(B) ignominious – shameful and degrading; debasing

(C) opprobrious – contemptuous, scornful, abusive

(D) terse – brief and to the point

(E) equivocal – deliberately misleading; vague

(F) laconic – using few words; terse

The correct answers would be 'ignominious' and 'opprobrious'. The words 'mundane' and 'equivocal' are not relevant to the context of the sentence. 'Terse' and 'equivocal' can be debated to be close but in actuality their contextual meaning of 'being brief' is not the central focus of this sentence: it is not the briefness of the title that was its defining quality. These, therefore, do not match the context of the sentence.

The correct answers are B & C.

45. Let us understand the meaning of the sentence from the partial information.

It states that she had desired for long to visit Spain, but her first reaction was **a particular** type and this contrasted the fact that she had been longing for a long time to visit the place. The **hint-phrase** here is **yearned for so long**. This is acted on by the signal-phrase "**contrasted sharply with**". Therefore the word **indifferent** will be the **fill-in**.

Let us pre-empt the **fill-in**; it should be a relatable word from the synonym family of **indifferent**.

Let us understand the meanings of the option words.

(A) disconsolate – hopelessly unhappy; sad beyond consolation

(B) ecstatic – joyful and filled with delight

(C) tepid – not enthusiastic; halfhearted

(D) apathetic – showing or feeling no interest, enthusiasm, or concern

(E) enraptured – joyful and filled with delight

(F) sinister – evil or criminal

The correct answers would be 'tepid' and 'apathetic'. The words 'ecstatic' and 'enraptured' are opposites of what the context requires. The word 'sinister' does not fit the context. The word 'disconsolate' brings a negative undertone and seems like a fit, but a closer evaluation of its meaning reveals that it brings the context of extreme unhappiness to the point of hopelessness: this is not present in the context of the sentence. 'Disconsolate', therefore, is not in line with what the sentence requires.

The correct answers are C & D.

46. Let us understand the meaning of the sentence from the partial information.

It describes the current trend of how Impressionist art is now making its way into the mainstream and that it was once considered strange and was found only in the homes of rich **somebodies** who spent time on such things that were unfamiliar to the common man. The **hint-word** here is **esoteric**, this describes the somebodies. We therefore know that these people knew about and invested time on things that very few other people cared or knew about. There is no specific simple word that can be used for the **fill-in** here.

Let us pre-empt the **fill-in**; it should be relatable words that brings the context of 'people interested in unfamiliar things'.

Let us understand the meanings of the option words.

(A) philistines – boorish and uncultured people

(B) cognoscenti – people with superior, usually specialized knowledge or highly refined taste; connoisseurs

(C) connoisseurs – people who have expert knowledge, especially in the fine arts

(D) initiates – people who have just been introduced into a particular field

(E) lowbrows – people who have uncultivated or nonintellectual tastes

(F) fledglings – young or inexperience people

The correct answers would be 'cognoscenti' and 'connoisseurs' since they both bring in the context of people who have expert knowledge in things unfamiliar by the common people: this relates to the hint-word 'esoteric'. The words 'philistines' and 'lowbrows' are contrasting to the context of the sentence as it refers to people who do not appreciate the arts or refinement. The words 'initiates' and 'fledglings' do not match the context of the sentence.

The correct answers are B & C.

47. Let us understand the meaning of the sentence from the partial information.

It states that Djindjic will be remembered as **somebody**: he sold out his country to enemies to benefit himself. The **hint-phrase** here is **"enriched himself by selling his country"**. The word **traitor** can act as the **fill-in** here.

Let us pre-empt the **fill-in**; it should be a relatable word from the synonym family of **traitor**.

Let us understand the meanings of the option words.

(A) pyromaniac – person with a mania for setting things on fire

(B) quisling – traitor who aids an occupying enemy force

(C) chauvinist – person with a prejudiced belief in the superiority of his or her own kind

(D) malingerer – person who shirks duty by faking illness

(E) treasonist – person who betrays his country by committing treason

(F) skulker – person who shirks duty by faking illness

The correct answers would be 'quisling' and 'treasonist'. The words 'pyromaniac', 'malingerer' and 'skulker' do not fit the context of the sentence. 'Chauvinist' brings the meaning of being overly patriotic about one's country (in this case) and is therefore contrary to the context required by the sentence.

The correct answers are B & E.

48. Let us understand the meaning of the sentence from the partial information.

It states that Jillian was considered **something** by her friend and family, and that this was in contrast to how her parents were (calm and steady). The **hint-phrase** here is **'resolve and tranquility'**. The **signal-phrase 'in contrast to'** suggests that she was known to be quite opposite to how her parents were. The **fill-in** must be opposite to the word 'stable' or 'calm' and therefore **'unpredictable'** could fit.

Let us pre-empt the **fill-in**; it should be a relatable word from the synonym family of **'unpredictable'**.

Let us understand the meanings of the option words.

(A) introverted – interested in or preoccupied with oneself or one's own thoughts as opposed to others or the environment; shy or reserved

(B) phlegmatic – calm and sluggish in temperament; unemotional or apathetic

(C) mercurial – quick and changeable in temperament; volatile

(D) mendacious – lying; untruthful

(E) explosive – likely to lead to violence or hostility

(F) taciturn – habitually untalkative

The correct answers would be 'mercurial' and 'explosive'. The words 'introverted', 'phlegmatic' and 'taciturn' are sort of contrasting in context as they bring a meaning of being quiet and withdrawn. 'Mendacious' does not fit the context of the sentence.

The correct answers are C & E.

49. Let us understand the meaning of the sentence from the partial information.

It describes the German painter's view towards **something**; it states that he finds **something** repulsive or disgusting. The **hint-words** here are that his work invites high-flown comparisons and that he is suspicious of anything that romanticizes the creative art. These words suggest that he hates exaggeration; this will be the **fill-in.**

Let us pre-empt the **fill-in**; it should be a relatable word from the synonym family of **exaggeration.**

Let us understand the meanings of the option words.

(A) cynicism – scorn and jaded negativity

(B) aggrandizement – exaggeration; attempt at making something appear greater than it really is

(C) skepticism – doubt or disbelief

(D) antipathy – extreme dislike; aversion

(E) apathy – lack of interest, enthusiasm, or concern

(F) hyperbole – obvious or intentional exaggeration

The correct answers would be 'aggrandizement' and 'hyperbole'. The words 'cynicism', 'skepticism', 'antipathy', and 'apathy' do not fit the context of the sentence.

The correct answers are B & F.

50. Let us understand the meaning of the sentence from the partial information.

It states that the austerity measures taken to do **something** to advanced economies' fiscal weakness may also actually affect their growth. There is no clear **hint-phrase** here but the context of the sentence can give us an idea: 'austerity measures' are those taken to reduce spending and excess waste, therefore, their role would be to heal or fix their fiscal weakness. The **fill-in** can therefore be **'fix'.**

Let us pre-empt the fill-in; it should be relatable words that brings the context of **'fix'.**

Let us understand the meanings of the option words.

(A) extenuate – lessen the seriousness or extent of something

(B) cull – pick out and put aside the inferior of a population

(C) increase – increase in extent

(D)   amplify – make larger or more powerful; increase

(E)   mitigate – make less severe or intense; alleviate

(F)   decimate – kill or destroy a large population of something

The correct answers would be 'extenuate' and 'mitigate'. 'Increase' and 'amplify' are opposites of what is required in context. The words 'cull' and 'decimate' are not relevant in context.

The correct answers are A & E.

51.   Let us understand the meaning of the sentence from the partial information.

It describes the child one who felt more like a naughty and ill-tempered child as his **something** increased. The **hint-phrase** here is "**felt more like a naughty and ill-tempered child**". The phrase **ill temper** can work as the **fill-in**.

Let us pre-empt the **fill-in**; it should be a relatable word that brings the context of **ill temper**.

Let us understand the meanings of the option words.

(A)   peevishness – an irritable disposition

(B)   caprice – sudden, unaccountable change of mood or behavior

(C)   petulance – bad tempered and childishly sulky

(D)   solemnness – deep sincerity; seriousness

(E)   sedateness – calmness, sedateness and unhurriedness

(F)   nescience – ignorance

The correct answers would be 'peevishness' and 'petulance'. The word 'caprice', although similar to the **fill-in** does brings the context of 'fickleness', which is not really relevant in this sentence. In the absence of either 'peevishness' or 'petulance', it would have been a preferred choice. The words 'solemnness', 'sedateness' and 'nescience' do not match the context of the sentence.

The correct answers are A & C.

52.   Let us understand the meaning of the sentence from the partial information.

It states that it is well known that children, as they are developing into adults, are easily influenced; yet, their **something** at certain situations is nonetheless surprising. We know that the **hint-word** here is **impressionable**. The **signal phrases 'Even though'** and '**nevertheless surprising**' act on each other to suggest that even though the behavior is well known, that they would behave the same way (to an extreme extent) in certain scenarios seems surprising. The phrase **gullibility** can act as the **fill-in**.

Let us pre-empt the **fill-in**; it should be a relatable word that brings the context of **gullibility**.

Let us understand the meanings of the option words.

(A)   gaucheness – social awkwardness

(B)   credulity – a disposition to believe too readily

(C) tactlessness – lacking skill or sensitivity when dealing with others

(D) disingenuousness – not straightforward or candid; insincere

(E) naiveté – lack of experience, wisdom or judgment

(F) artfulness – cleverness or skillfulness, especially in crafty or cunning ways

The correct answers would be 'credulity' and 'naiveté' since they both bring the context of 'gullibility'. The words 'disingenuousness' and 'artfulness' bring the context of being 'cunning' and 'deceptive' and are sort of opposites of what is required in this sentence. The words 'gaucheness' and 'tactlessness' do not match the context of the sentence.

The correct answers are B & E.

53. Let us understand the meaning of the sentence from the partial information.

It states that even after his attempts to **do something to** her beliefs about him, she remained very fixed in her former opinion. The **hint-phrases** here are '**remained stubborn in her opinion**' and '**His attempts…were futile**'. The meaning conveyed is that he tried to change her belief or correct her preconceptions about him. The **fill-in** here would be **rectify**.

Let us pre-empt the **fill-in**; it should be a relatable word that brings the context of **rectify**.

Let us understand the meanings of the option words.

(A) castigate – punish or rebuke severely

(B) condone – overlook, forgive or disregard

(C) excoriate – criticize harshly

(D) disabuse – free from a falsehood or misconception

(E) undeceive – tell someone that an idea or belief is mistaken

(F) exonerate – free from blame

The correct answers would be 'disabuse' and 'undeceive'. The words 'castigate' and 'excoriate' are extreme and there are no contextual hints to support this in the sentence. The words 'condone' and 'exonerate' bring the meaning of 'forgive' or 'overlook faults', which is not supported by the context of the sentence.

The correct answers are D & E.

54. Let us understand the meaning of the sentence from the partial information.

It describes the community suggesting that although it is generally considered a farming community, the perception is wrong: the **something** of the resident's occupation makes the classification of "primarily farming" inaccurate. The **hint-words** here are **primarily** and **antiquated**. Along with the signal word **although** we realize that this community actually has a large number of different occupations and therefore calling it a 'primarily farming' community would be wrong. The word '**wide range of**' will be our **fill-in**.

Let us pre-empt the **fill-in**; it should be a relatable word that brings the context of '**wide range of**'.

Let us understand the meanings of the option words.

(A) profitability – quality of yielding profit or financial gain

(B) productivity – quality of achieving significant amount of result

(C) diversity – range of different things

(D) fecundity – ability to produce in abundance

(E) heterogeneity – diversity in character or content

(F) stability – secure; steady

The correct answers would be 'diversity' and 'heterogeneity'. The words 'profitability' and 'stability' do not match the context of the sentence. The words 'productivity' and 'fecundity' do not bring the meaning of 'wide range of' and are therefore not relevant in the context.

The correct answers are C & E.

55. Let us understand the meaning of the sentence from the partial information.

It states that **something** within state-owned companies has not let them distribute the prosperity in a just and equal way. The **hint-phrase** here can be found in the latter part of the sentence: "**has prevented a more equitable distribution of prosperity**". The phrase '**unfair practices**' could work as a **fill-in**.

Let us pre-empt the **fill-in**; it should be a relatable word that brings the context of '**unfair practices**'.

Let us understand the meanings of the option words.

(A) Chicanery – Use of deception or subterfuge to achieve one's purpose

(B) Bureaucracy – Excessively complicated administrative procedure

(C) Regimentation – Organization according to a strict system or pattern

(D) Unscrupulousness – Dishonesty; without moral principles

(E) Hierarchy – A system in which members of an organization or society are ranked according to relative status or authority

(F) Regulation – Control by means of rules

The correct answers would be 'chicanery' and 'unscrupulousness' since these are contextually relevant to 'unfair practices'. The words 'regimentation' and 'regulation' do not fit the context as they, if implemented, should only improve the overall 'fairness' of the company. The words 'bureaucracy' and 'hierarchy' may seem possible but they do not bring in the context of 'unfairness' and are therefore not relevant; they may hamper the progress of companies, but not necessarily affect distribution of prosperity.

The correct answers are A & D.

56. Let us understand the meaning of the sentence from the partial information.

It states that the movie '*Side Effects*' although with an original screenplay serves as the director's departing or final work since it brings together in **particular** form many of the elements from the director's past works. The **hint-phrases** here are **original screenplay**, **valedictory work** and **brings together**. The signal word **although** works with **original screenplay** to suggest that there are elements of older works captured in this movie. The word **summarizing** could work as a **fill-in**.

Let us pre-empt the **fill-in**; it should be a relatable word that brings the context of **summarizing**.

Let us understand the meanings of the option words.

(A) synoptic – presenting a summary or a general view of the whole

(B) curbed – restrained; kept in check

(C) restrained – kept under control

(D) investigative – intensively inquiring

(E) précised – summarized or abstracted

(F) melodramatic – sensationally dramatic; overly exaggerated

The correct answers would be 'synoptic' and 'précised' since they being in the context of 'summarizing'. The word 'curbed' and 'restrained' share the meaning of 'constraining information' but they also have a negative undertone that does not fit the context of the sentence. The word 'investigative' and 'melodramatic' are not relevant to the context of the sentence.

The correct answers are A & E.

57. Let us understand the meaning of the sentence from the partial information.

It describes the current trend of news reporting and reader behavior and states that most news reports are **something**: they are quickly forgotten. The sentence also states that for a report to not be forgotten quickly it has to be exceptional.

The **hint-phrases** here are '**forgotten before fully assimilated**' and '**to have any type of permanence…**'. Based on these phrases it is clear that news reports are generally **short-lived** since they have to be exceptional to achieve any type of permanence.

Let us pre-empt the **fill-in**; it should be a relatable word that brings the context of **short-lived**.

Let us understand the meanings of the option words.

(A) ephemeral – lasting a very short time

(B) donnish – bookish or pedantic

(C) parochial – have a limited or narrow outlook

(D) evanescent – vanishing; fading away

(E) pedantic – excessively concerned with minor details or rules

(F) insular – circumscribed and detached in outlook and experience

The correct answers would be 'ephemeral' and 'evanescent'. The words 'donnish' and 'pedantic' do not match the context of the sentence. The words 'parochial' and 'insular' may seem relevant, but on closer inspection of their meaning we realize that it means to have a 'limited scope of influence' and has no relevance to the context of the sentence, which is 'short-lived'.

The correct answers are A & D.

58. Let us understand the meaning of the sentence from the partial information.

It states what current research on development psychology suggests about stressful ex-periences during infancy: these stressful experiences, it says, are essential for normal emotional growth and they are not an indicative sign of future problems in childhood or **something** of the onset of problems when the child becomes a teen. The **hint-word** here is **herald** and we realize that this is paralleled in the latter part of the sentence as well. Therefore, the word **predict** can act as the fill-in.

Let us pre-empt the **fill-in**; it should be a relatable word that brings the context of **predict**.

Let us understand the meanings of the option words.

(A) forestall – prevent or obstruct by taking action in advance

(B) augur – portend a good or bad outcome

(C) foil – prevent from succeeding

(D) portend – be a sign of warning that something is about to happen

(E) vitiate – spoil or impair the efficiency or quality of

(F) maculate – mark with spots; stain

The correct answers would be 'augur' and 'portend'. The words 'forestall' and 'foil' are in someway opposites of what the context requires. The words 'vitiate' and 'maculate' do not fit the context of the sentence.

The correct answers are B & D.

59. Let us understand the meaning of the sentence from the partial information.

It states that Tim Roth's performance, while cheered on by the audience did not feel authentic because the way he portrayed himself onstage seemed a **particular** way. The hint-phrase here is '**didn't feel authentic**'. This must have made his persona onstage seem **fake** or **not genuine**.

Let us pre-empt the **fill-in**; it should be a relatable word that brings the context of **not genuine**.

Let us understand the meanings of the option words.

(A) spontaneous – arising from a natural inclination or impulse and not from fore-thought or prompting

(B) contrived – artificial and unrealistic

(C) candid – truthful and straightforward; frank

(D) gaudy – extravagantly bright and showy

(E) affected – pretentious and designed to impress; artificial

(F) garish – overly bright or ornamental; gaudy

The correct answers would be 'contrived' and 'affected' as they bring in the context of being 'not genuine' or 'fake'. The words 'spontaneous' and 'candid' bring the context of being 'authentic' and are therefore opposites of what the context requires. The words 'gaudy' and 'garish' may seem relevant but they do not convey the meaning of being 'not genuine' or 'fake' and are therefore not relevant to the context of the sentence.

The correct answers are B & E.

60. Let us understand the meaning of the sentence from the partial information.

It states that Mr. Berkley, by appearing in **some kind of** camp, caused the people to get angry. The hint-phrase here is "**without any real intention to bolster relief efforts but rather intended just for the cameras**". The word "**a fake**" will be the **fill-in**.

Let us pre-empt the **fill-in**; it should be a relatable word that brings the context of "**a fake**".

Let us understand the meanings of the option words.

(A) an evitable – avoidable

(B) a celluloid – synthetic; fake

(C) an ersatz – artificial; fake

(D) a congruous – corresponding in character and kind

(E) a simpatico – like minded; compatible

(F) an exigent – urgent; requiring immediate action

The correct answers would be 'a celluloid' and 'a ersatz'. The words 'an evitable', 'a congruous', 'a simpatico' and 'an exigent' do not match the context of the sentence.

The correct answers are B & C.

61. Let us understand the meaning of the sentence from the partial information.

It describes medicine's current perspective on treatments: that surgery should be avoided. The sentence then describes the resultant focus on treatments that postpone and sometimes even completely **do something** to the need for surgery.

The **hint-phrase** in this sentence is "**often postpone, and sometimes even completely...**". Based on this we realize that these treatments, in some cases, might make surgery unnecessary. The word **make unnecessary** can act as the **fill-in**.

Let us pre-empt the **fill-in**; it should be a relatable word that brings the context of **make unnecessary**.

Let us understand the meanings of the option words.

(A) expedite – speed up the process or execute quickly

(B) trivialize – make or cause to appear unimportant or of little value

(C) obviate – render unnecessary; keep something from happening

(D) vilify – attack the reputation of someone with strong or abusive criticism

(E) forefend – prevent something from happening

(F) precipitate – cause something to happen suddenly or prematurely

The correct answers would be 'obviate' and 'forefend'. The words 'expedite' and 'precipitate' bring the meaning of 'making something happen quicker' and this is in contrast with what the sentence requires. The words 'trivialize' and 'vilify' seem relevant, but on close analysis of their meaning we realize that they mean to 'talk lowly about' something. This is not in line with the context of 'make unnecessary' and therefore they do not fit the context of the sentence.

The correct answers are C & E.

62. Let us understand the meaning of the sentence from the partial information.

It states Nicky Romero's suggestion about his art: that the artistic intricacies in his music is **something**: not easily understood by people who have normal levels of artistic appreciation. The **hint-phrase** here is '**closed to the average enthusiast**'. This suggests that only some very specialized set of people would be able to truly appreciate his music. The phase '**not understood by many**' will be the **fill-in**.

Let us pre-empt the **fill-in**; it should be a relatable word that brings the context of **not understood by many**.

Let us understand the meanings of the option words.

(A) intuitive – easily understood and simple to use

(B) elementary – not difficult; simple

(C) unreliable – not reliable; untrustworthy

(D) visceral – arising from impulse or sudden emotion rather than from thought or deliberation

(E) recondite – known or understood by relatively few

(F) arcane – known or understood by only a few

The correct answers would be 'recondite' and 'arcane'. The words 'intuitive' and 'elementary' mean to be 'easily understood' and are therefore opposites of what the context requires. The words 'unreliable' and 'visceral' do not fit the context of the sentence.

The correct answers are E & F.

63. Let us understand the meaning of the sentence from the partial information.

It states that some voters have not been happy with Holland's participation in the bailout of European countries since it rewards **some type** of countries while the Dutch have to live a life of strict simplicity, without luxuries or comfort. The **hint-word austerity** and the signal word **while** gives us a perspective on the kind of countries the sentence discusses. The word '**overly spending**' or '**wasteful**' can act as the **fill-in**.

Let us pre-empt the **fill-in**; it should be a relatable word that brings the context of **wasteful**.

Let us understand the meanings of the option words.

(A) incompetent – incapable of performing a particular task

(B) inept – unskillful; incompetent

(C) profligate – recklessly wasteful; wildly extravagant

(D) judicious – prudent; having sound judgment

(E) circumspect – cautious or prudent

(F) prodigal – recklessly wasteful or extravagant

The correct answers would be 'profligate' and 'prodigal'. The words 'judicious' and 'circumspect' are contrary to the sentence requires. The words 'incompetent' and 'inept', although negative words, bring in the meaning of 'without skill or competence' and do not necessarily mean to be 'wasteful'; they are therefore not relevant to the context of the sentence.

The correct answers are C & F.

64. Let us understand the meaning of the sentence from the partial information.

It states that the title 'engineer' has been broadly used in the IT world that its meaning has become almost something. The **hint-phrase** here is '**has been used so broadly**'. The word **non-specific** or **unclear** could act as the **fill-in**.

Let us pre-empt the **fill-in**; it should be a relatable word that brings the context of **unclear**.

Let us understand the meanings of the option words.

(A) pejorative – expressive of disapproval; derogatory

(B) indistinct – not clearly or sharply defined

(C) derogatory – intended to belittle; intended to be intentionally offensive

(D) blurred – unclear in form or expression

(E) acceptable – satisfactory; adequate

(F) convenient – easy to use

The correct answers would be 'indistinct' and 'blurred'. The words 'pejorative' and 'derogatory' bring in the context of 'belittling' or showing 'disapproval'; this is not supported by the context of the sentence. The words 'acceptable' and 'convenient' do not match the context of 'unclear' that the sentence requires.

The correct answers are B & D.

65. Let us understand the meaning of the sentence from the partial information.

It states that since ego and selflessness are opposites but found in the same individuals; they mutually **do something** to each other. The **hint-phrases** here are **diametrically different** and **but not necessarily destroy one another**. This suggests that the two entities act on each other to reduce each others' influence, yet not to the extent to destroy each other. The word **weaken** can act as the fill-in.

Let us understand the meanings of the option words.

(A) reinforce – strengthen or support with additional material

(B) annihilate – destroy utterly; obliterate

(C) enhance – intensify; improve or increase the quality of something

(D) attenuate – reduce the force or effect of

(E) decimate – kill or destroy a large population of

(F) dampen – make less strong or intense

The correct answers would be 'attenuate' and 'dampen'. The words 'reinforce' and 'enhance' have a positive undertone and are opposites of what the sentence requires. The words 'annihilate' and 'decimate' mean to 'destroy'; the sentence explicitly suggests that they do not destroy each other. Thus, the word 'annihilate' and 'decimate' are not in line with what the sentence requires.

The correct answers are D & F.

66. Let us understand the meaning of the sentence from the partial information.

It states that although Jolene felt hurt, she did not react in a way that showed her feelings. Although, her calmness was due to her keeping in **something** the extremes of her emotions rather than her not feeling anything at all. The **hint-phrases** here are '**her words were not without emotion**', '**retained her composure**' and '**extremes of sentiments**'. This suggests that she felt very extreme emotions, yet retained her composure. The word **balance** could work as the **fill-in**.

Let us pre-empt the **fill-in**; it should be a relatable word that brings the context of **balance**.

Let us understand the meanings of the option words.

(A) limit – a state of restriction

(B) equilibrium – a condition in which all acting influences are canceled by others, resulting in a stable, balanced, or unchanging system.

(C) friction – a state of conflict

(D) oscillation – the act of swinging between two extremes

(E) subjection – forced submission to control by others

(F) equipoise – even balance of emotional forces; equilibrium

The correct answers would be 'equilibrium' and 'equipoise'. The word 'oscillation' suggests switching between two extremes. This would not fit the context, as she did not switch between the extremes: she found a balance between them. The word 'limit' and 'subjection' suggests 'controlling one's feelings'; a close reading of the text suggests that she did not really control her feelings, rather found 'balance'. Hence these words do not match the context of the sentence. The word 'friction' is in contrast to the context of the sentence.

The correct answers are B & F.

67. Let us understand the meaning of the sentence from the partial information.

It states that the book Ulysses has several editions, yet all of them are **particular** types of versions. They are altered or tweaked to suit a family or domestic kind of readership. The hint-phrase here is '**adapted to suit a predominantly family and domestic readership**'. The phrase '**adapted to be suitable for families**' makes sense here: the word '**censored**', therefore, will be the **fill-in**.

Let us pre-empt the **fill-in**; it should be a relatable word that brings the context of **censored**.

Let us understand the meanings of the option words.

(A) censured – severely criticized

(B) transcribed – data, speech or thoughts put in written form

(C) expurgated – removed of matter thought to be objectionable or unsuitable

(D) reproofed – severely criticized; expressed disapproval of

(E) impounded – seized and taken legal custody of

(F) bowdlerized – removed of material that is considered inappropriate or offensive

The correct answers would be 'expurgated' and 'bowdlerized'. The words 'censured', 'transcribed', 'reproofed' and 'impounded' do not fit the context of the sentence.

The correct answers are C & F.

68. Let us understand the meaning of the sentence from the partial information.

It states that the sculpture was made to look a **particular** way because of the way it was displayed: in a dark corner of the museum. The **hint-phrase** here is '**Larger than it appeared to be**' suggesting that the sculpture was made to look smaller by the perspective. The phrase '**made to look smaller**' will act as the **fill-in**.

Let us pre-empt the **fill-in**; it should be a relatable word that brings the context of **made to look smaller**.

Let us understand the meanings of the option words.

(A) aggrandized – made larger in status or wealth

(B) diminished – made to seem small or less impressive

(C) embellished – made more attractive by adding decorative details or features

(D) substantiated – given proof to the truth

(E) dwarfed – made to seem smaller or insignificant

(F) ostracized – excluded from a group

The correct answers would be 'diminished' and 'dwarfed'. The words 'aggrandized' and 'embellished' bring a context of 'exaggeration' or 'making something look bigger'; this is in contrast with the context required by the sentence. The words 'substantiated' and 'ostracized' are not relevant to the context of the sentence.

The correct answers are B & E.

69. Let us understand the meaning of the sentence from the partial information.

It states that interacting with a world by mostly shooting things is very limiting and a particular game maker used this limitation to make a point that violence is **something**. The **hint-phrase** is '**that people who have no option but violence are ultimately powerless**'. This suggests that violence has no apparent effect and is quite pointless. The word '**useless**' can act as the **fill-in**.

Let us pre-empt the **fill-in**; it should be a relatable word that brings the context of **useless**.

Let us understand the meanings of the option words.

(A) imperative – of vital importance

(B) edifying – enlightening or uplifting so as to encourage intellectual or moral improvement

(C) futile – incapable of producing any useful result

(D) vain – producing no result; useless

(E) gratifying – pleasing to the mind or feeling

(F) inexorable – impossible to stop or resist; inevitable

The correct answers would be 'futile' and 'vain'. The words 'imperative' and 'inexorable' are sort of contrary to the context that the sentence requires as they suggest that violence is 'important' or 'unavoidable'. Similarly, 'edifying' and 'gratifying' suggest a positive correlation with violence, which the sentence does not support.

The correct answers are C & D.

70. Let us understand the meaning of the sentence from the partial information.

It states that Henry VIII was called a **someone** of science because he provided generous financial support to many young scientists. The phrase '**provided generous financial support**' acts as the **hint-phrase** and suggests that he was a supported of the sciences. The word **supporter** can act as the **fill-in**.

Let us pre-empt the **fill-in**; it should be a relatable word that brings the context of **supporter**.

Let us understand the meanings of the option words.

(A) disparager – one who belittles the worth of something

(B) champion – a person who supports or defends a cause

(C) detractor – one who belittles the worth of something

(D) patron – a person who supports something with money, effort or endorsement

(E) regent – one who rules during the minority, absence, or disability of a monarch

(F) demagogue – a person who gains power by arousing people's emotions and prejudices

The correct answers would be 'champion' and 'patron'. The words 'disparager' and 'detractor' convey a meaning that is in contrast to context required by the sentence. The words 'regent' and 'demagogue' refer types of rulers, but this isn't the focus of the sentence, furthermore the words do not bring in the context of being a 'supporter' of the sciences.

The correct answers are B & D.

71. Let us understand the meaning of the sentence from the partial information.

It states that premature rate growth could do **something** to the problems of high unemployment and weak wage growth in America. There is no specific **hint-word** in this sentence; but the entire of the sentence provides a context to help us preempt a **fill-in**. The word '**premature**' suggests a negative outcome; therefore, this might only work to worsening the problems. The word **worsen** will act as the **fill-in**.

Let us pre-empt the **fill-in**; it should be a relatable word that brings the context of **worsen**.

Let us understand the meanings of the option words.

(A) exacerbate – increase the severity, violence or bitterness

(B) mollify – calm anger; soothe or appease

(C) eliminate – get rid of; remove

(D) aggravate – make worse

(E) palliate – make less severe or intense

(F) eradicate – get rid of; eliminate

The correct answers would be 'exacerbate' and 'aggravate'. The words 'mollify' and 'palliate' are opposites of what the context requires. The words 'eliminate' and 'eradicate' in context would bring in a positive outcome and this is also contrary to what the sentence requires.

The correct answers are A & D.

72. Let us understand the meaning of the sentence from the partial information.

It states that poets who came from other lands sang praises in a form that was a **particular**, overloaded poetry. The **hint-phrases** here are '**overloaded poetry**' and '**with little real feeling**'. The latter part of the sentence provides further information showing contrast (through the signal word '**In contrast**') with the women singers at course who '**sang poetry that was full of natural feeling, simple in language and moving in content**'. The poetry of the outsiders therefore was probably '**overly complex and intended to look fancy**'; this can act as the **fill-in**.

Let us pre-empt the **fill-in**; it should be a relatable word that brings the context of '**overly complex and intended to look fancy**'.

Let us understand the meanings of the option words.

(A) grandiloquent – pompous or boastful speech or expression

(B) pithy – precisely meaningful; forceful and brief

(C) perfidious – guilty, treacherous, or faithless; deceitful

(D) laconic – using few words; terse or concise

(E) pompous – full of high-sounding phrases; bombastic

(F) duplicitous – deliberately deceptive behavior or speech

The correct answers would be 'grandiloquent' and 'pompous' as only these words bring the context of 'overly complex and intended to impress'. The words 'pithy' and 'laconic' are opposites of what is required in context. The words 'perfidious' and 'duplicitous' can mean to be 'deceptive' and although the sentence seems to support this, a closer evaluation of their meanings reveals that these words bring a negative undertone with a context of 'treachery'; this cannot be supported by the context of the sentence.

The correct answers are A & E.

73. Let us understand the meaning of the sentence from the partial information.

It states that few did **something** to the character of the President, yet they abused and spoke badly about his administration. The sentence draws a parallel between two entities: the President and his administration and the signal-word **yet** shows that these two were treated different attitudes. The **hint-word** here is **vilified**. Therefore, few ventured to **vilify** or **talk badly about** the president; 'talk against' can work as the **fill-in**.

Let us pre-empt the **fill-in**; it should be a relatable word that brings the context of **talk badly about**.

Let us understand the meanings of the option words.

(A) bespangle – make more attractive by adding ornament, color, etc.

(B) asperse – spread false or damaging accusations or insinuations against (someone)

(C) demystify – make less mysterious; clarify

(D) endorse – express approval of or give support to, especially by public statement; sanction

(E) obfuscate – make so confused or opaque as to be difficult to perceive or understand

(F) besmirch – stain; sully; damage; tarnish

The correct answers would be 'asperse' and 'besmirch' since these words bring in the context of 'speaking or doing something bad about someone'. The words 'bespangle' and 'endorse' are opposites of what the context requires. The words 'demystify' and 'obfuscate' do not match the context of the sentence.

The correct answers are B & F.

74. Let us understand the meaning of the sentence from the partial information.

It states that people have a benign view of dementia, yet it has a more **some type** of side. The hint-phrase here is '**sufferers become aggressive and more difficult to care for**'. The word '**violent**' or '**aggressive**' can work as the **fill-in**.

Let us pre-empt the **fill-in**; it should be a relatable word that brings the context of **violent**.

Let us understand the meanings of the option words.

(A) truculent – eager or quick to argue or fight; aggressively defiant

(B) eloquent – fluent or persuasive in speaking or writing

(C) placid – not easily upset; calm and peaceful

(D) prolix – using or containing too many words; tediously lengthy

(E) pugnacious – eager or quick to argue, quarrel, or fight

(F) tranquil – free from disturbance; calm

The correct answers would be 'truculent' and 'pugnacious'. The words 'placid' and 'tranquil' mean to be peaceful; this is opposite to what the context requires. The words 'eloquent' and 'prolix' are not relevant to the context of the sentence.

The correct answers are A & E.

75. Let us understand the meaning of the sentence from the partial information.

It discusses what Fredric says in his essay; that in England while agnosticism was treated with tolerance and even considered fashionable, atheism was treaded with **something**. The signal word **while** contrasts shows that the **fill-in** is in contrast to the **hint-phrase** '**fashionable**'. Therefore atheism was probably treated with **hate** or **disapproval**; this will act as the fill-in.

Let us pre-empt the **fill-in**; it should be a relatable word that brings the context of **disapproval**.

Let us understand the meanings of the option words.

(A) obloquy – disgrace, especially that brought about by public condemnation

(B) accolade – award or privilege granted to show praise or admiration

(C) apathy – lack of interest, enthusiasm or concern

(D) approbation – approval or praise

(E) passiveness – acceptance or something that happens or what others do, without active response or resistance

(F) calumny – false and defamatory statements about someone made in order to damage their reputation; slander

The correct answers would be 'obloquy' and 'calumny'; although these words don't directly mean 'disapproval' they bring the context of 'showing dislike or hate for something' and therefore are relevant to the context of the sentence. The words 'accolade' and 'approbation' have a positive undertone and are therefore in contrast with what the sentence requires. The words 'apathy' and 'passiveness' may seem relevant, but on close examination of their meanings, we realize that they don't mean 'hate' or disapproval'; the degree to which 'obloquy' and 'calumny' convey the intended meaning is not served with 'apathy' and 'passiveness'.

The correct answers are A & F.

76. Let us understand the meaning of the sentence from the partial information.

It describes his belief about a certain person; he believed that she was extremely open and frank and therefore refused to accept the possibility that what she said had been **something**. The **hint-phrase** here is found in the first part of the sentence '**she possessed great integrity and candor**'. The signal-phrase '**he therefore refused to consider the possibility...**' suggests a contrasting quality that she might possess. The word **untrue** can work as the **fill-in**.

Let us pre-empt the **fill-in**; it should be a relatable word that brings the context of **untrue**.

Let us understand the meanings of the option words.

(A) insincere – not expressing genuine feelings

(B) fatuous – silly and pointless

(C) facetious – treating serious issues with deliberate inappropriate humor

(D) irrelevant – not relevant to something

(E) inconsequential – not important or significant

(F) disingenuous – not candid or sincere

The correct answers would be 'insincere' and 'disingenuous', both of these words bring in a meaning that is opposite to the word 'sincere' and are also in line with the **fill-in** 'untrue'. The words 'irrelevant' and 'inconsequential' do not match the context of 'untrue'. The words 'fatuous' and 'facetious' bring the meaning of being 'unserious deliberately' and though might seem relevant in context – do not really bring in the meaning of being 'untrue' or 'not sincere'.

The correct answers are A & F.

77. Let us understand the meaning of the sentence from the partial information.

It states that The Hegel reader is well renounced because it makes clear and understandable many of Hegel's **particular** kind of philosophical concepts. The **hint-phrases** here are '**it clarifies many of…**' and '**which have been considered abstract by even the most perspicacious scholars**'. This suggests that the book simplifies things that were considered almost impossible to understand by many. The phrase '**difficult to understand**' can act as the **fill-in**.

Let us pre-empt the **fill-in**; it should be a relatable word that brings the context of **difficult to understand**.

Let us understand the meanings of the option words.

(A) inscrutable – impossible to understand or interpret

(B) insidious – proceeding in gradual, subtle way, but with very harmful effects

(C) sophomoric – pretentious or juvenile

(D) ignominious – deserving or causing public disgrace or shame

(E) impenetrable – impossible to understand

(F) nugatory – of no value or importance

The correct answers would be 'inscrutable' and 'impenetrable'. The words 'insidious' and 'ignominious' are not relevant to the context of the sentence. The words 'sophomoric' and 'nugatory' suggest a quality of 'lacking value or quality' does not match the context required by the sentence.

The correct answers are A & E.

78. Let us understand the meaning of the sentence from the partial information.

It describes the photographic style of Lauren. It says that her pictures lacked polish and had a **something** that captured the causal and relaxed spirit of her generation. The hint-phrase, found in the latter part of the sentence is, '**nonchalant spirit**'. The word '**relaxed**' can work as the **fill-in**.

Let us pre-empt the **fill-in**; it should be a relatable word that brings the context of **relaxed**.

Let us understand the meanings of the option words.

(A) solemnity – serious and dignified quality

(B) insouciance – causal lack of concern

(C) graveness – serious and solemn quality

(D) animosity – strong hostility

(E) carefreeness – lack of anxiety and responsibility

(F) malignancy – evil intentioned nature

The correct answers would be 'insouciance' and 'carefreeness' as they both bring in the context of 'lacking concern' and being 'relaxed'. The words 'animosity' and 'malignancy' are extremely negative words that suggest 'intending harm'; this does not match the required context of the sentence. The words 'solemnity' and 'graveness' are in contrast with the context of the sentence.

The correct answers are B & E.

79. Let us understand the meaning of the sentence from the partial information.

It states that Ms. Ziegelman hasn't just read through many cookbooks and newspapers thoroughly, but also has the ability to take out the most **some kind** of details from them. There are no clear **hint-words** here in this sentence, but the word '**admirable**' suggests that the details she must be picking should be ones that are very interesting or noteworthy. Therefore the word '**interesting**' can work as the **fill-in**.

Let us pre-empt the **fill-in**; it should be a relatable word that brings the context of **interesting**.

Let us understand the meanings of the option words.

(A) piquant – pleasantly stimulating or exciting to the mind

(B) acrimonious – angry and bitter

(C) tedious – tiresome or monotonous

(D) scathing – scornful; severely critical

(E) vivifying – lively or interesting

(F) monotonous – dull, tedious or repetitive

The correct answers would be 'piquant' and 'vivifying' since they both bring in the context of something being 'interesting'. The words 'acrimonious' and 'scathing' do not match the context of the sentence. The words 'tedious' and 'monotonous' are opposites of what the sentence requires.

The correct answers are A & E.

80. Let us understand the meaning of the sentence from the partial information.

It states that Jacques is known for his **some type of** collection. We know from the latter part of the sentence that his collection '**showcases a carried mix of antiquated furniture…**'; this is serves as the **hint-phrase**. The words **varied** or **diverse** can work as the fill-in.

Let us pre-empt the **fill-in**; it should be a relatable word that brings the context of **diverse**.

Let us understand the meanings of the option words.

(A) banal – lacking in originality; boring

(B) eclectic – derived from a diverse and broad range of sources

(C) baroque – highly ornate and extravagant

(D) refulgent – very brightly shining

(E) corpulent – fat

(F) catholic – including a wide variety of things

The correct answers would be 'eclectic' and 'catholic' since they both bring the meaning of 'diverse' or 'varied'. The words 'banal' has a negative undertone, which is not supported by the context of the sentence. The words 'baroque' and 'refulgent' mean to be 'very bright and gaudy'; the words may look relevant but there is contextual evidence to suggest that his collection was so. We only know that his collection was 'varied' or 'diverse'. The word 'corpulent' does not fit the context if the sentence.

The correct answers are B & F.

81. Let us understand the meaning of the sentence from the partial information.

It states that Kurgman points out that people shouldn't worry about inflation since in-flation not only has been **something** for years and that there's almost no chance it will return anytime soon. There is no direct **hint-word** here, but the context suggests that the current trend of how inflation has been will be an indicator of how it will be in the future. The word **'non-existent'** can be used as the **fill-in**.

Let us pre-empt the **fill-in**; it should be a relatable word that brings the context of **non-existent**.

Let us understand the meanings of the option words.

(A) rampant – unrestrained in action; spreading unchecked

(B) prestigious – inspiring respect and admiration

(C) ineluctable – unable to resist or avoid

(D) quiescent – in a state of inactivity; dormant

(E) pervasive – spreading widely throughout an area

(F) dormant – quiet and inactive; latent or inoperative

The correct answers would be 'quiescent' and 'dormant'; although these do not mean 'non-existent', these are the closest in meaning - and in context they suggest that in-flection has no existed for years. The words 'rampant' and 'pervasive' bring a context of 'wide spread' and this is in contrast with what the sentence requires. The word 'in-eluctable' also brings a meaning that will be opposite to what the context requires. The word 'prestigious' is not relevant to the context of the sentence.

The correct answers are D & F.

82. Let us understand the meaning of the sentence from the partial information.

It describes a person and details his qualities, showing contrasts in them: he is modest yet certain about his talents, anxious yet cool about his reputation and somehow both **something** and openly expressive without reservation about his influences. Apart from the contextual hint that shows contrasting qualities, the word **effusive** acts as a **hint-word**. The word **shy** can therefore work as the **fill-in** as it is contextually contrasting to **'effusive'**.

Let us pre-empt the **fill-in**; it should be a relatable word that brings the context of **shy**.

Let us understand the meanings of the option words.

(A) demure – reserved, modest and shy

(B) enthralled – fascinated and enthralled

(C) overt – done or shown openly

(D) reserved – slow to reveal emotion or opinion

(E) conspicuous – clearly visible

(F) enraptured – given to intense pleasure or joy

The correct answers would be 'demure' and 'reserved' as they are both contextually op-posite to the word 'effusive. The words 'overt' and 'conspicuous' are in contrast with what is required in the sentence. The words 'enthralled' and 'enraptured' are also in contrast to the context of the sentence since they suggest a meaning of 'open expression of joy'.

The correct answers are A & D.

83. Let us understand the meaning of the sentence from the partial information.

It states that while people of Turkey look forward to democratization, they fear the presidential candidate might amass power and become a **someone**. The hint-phrase here is '**concentrate all true power in his own hands**'. The word

dictator could be a suitable **fill-in**.

Let us pre-empt the **fill-in**; it should be a relatable word that brings the context of **dictator**.

Let us understand the meanings of the option words.

(A) demagogue –political leader who seeks support by appealing to popular desires and prejudices rather than by using rational argument.

(B) libertine – person, especially a man, who freely indulges in sensual pleasures without regard to moral

(C) despot – ruler or other person who holds absolute power

(D) autocrat – ruler who has absolute power

(E) connoisseur – expert judge in matters of taste

(F) hedonist – person who believes that the pursuit of pleasure is the most important thing in life; pleasure seeker

The correct answers would be 'despot' and 'autocrat'. The words 'libertine', 'connoisseur' and 'hedonist' do not match the context of the sentence. The word 'demagogue' does describe a type of ruler but it does not bring the context of 'someone with absolute power'.

The correct answers are C & D.

84. Let us understand the meaning of the sentence from the partial information.

It states that people wanted a Secretary of Defense who was tame and easily influenced, but that he became less **something** over time. The **hint-phrase** in this sentence is 'tame and amenable'. This combines with the signal-phrase '**became less**' to suggest that he became less tame and amenable. The word '**easily influenced**'

Let us pre-empt the **fill-in**; it should be a relatable word that brings the context of **easily influenced**.

Let us understand the meanings of the option words.

(A) indignant – feeling or showing anger or annoyance at what is perceived as unfair treatment

(B) pliant – easily directed or influenced; yielding

(C) recalcitrant – having an obstinately uncooperative attitude towards authority or discipline

(D) malleable – easily influenced; pliable

(E) refractory – stubborn or unmanageable

(F) chivalrous – courteous and gallant, especially towards women.

The correct answers would be 'pliant' and 'malleable'. The words 'indignant' and 'chivalrous' do not match the context of the sentence. The words 'recalcitrant' and 'refractory' are opposites of what the sentence requires.

The correct answers are B & D.

85. Let us understand the meaning of the sentence from the partial information.

It describes an especially **some kind of** campaign: it got very nasty and things got personal. The **hint-phrase 'marked by deeply personal allegations'** suggests that the campaign was especially unpleasant or disagreeable. The word **harsh** or **unpleasant** can act as the **fill-in**.

Let us pre-empt the **fill-in**; it should be a relatable word that brings the context of **harsh**.

Let us understand the meanings of the option words.

(A) gratifying – pleasing or satisfying

(B) rancorous – bitter and resentful

(C) endearing – inspiring affection

(D) ardent – very enthusiastic or passionate

(E) acrimonious – angry or bitter

(F) impassioned – filled with or showing great emotion

The correct answers would be 'rancorous' and 'acrimonious' since they both bring in the context of harsh and unpleasant. The words 'gratifying', 'endearing' and ardent' have a positive undertone to them, which is not supported by the context of the sentence. The word 'impassioned' suggests being overcome with emotion; while this is true of the sentence - the lack of a negative undertone or the contextual meaning 'unpleasant' or 'harsh' makes the word 'impassioned' not a good match for what the sentence requires.

The correct answers are B & E.

86. Let us understand the meaning of the sentence from the partial information.

It describes Solomon and states that he is slow in his development of abilities and that he is a bit socially **something**. There are no direct **hint-words** here but the context does provide us with some hints: 'late bloomer' and 'but this quality' suggests that Solomon's description must have a **negative undertone**. Since the context is socially **something**, the word **'awkward'** can act as the **fill-in**.

Let us pre-empt the **fill-in**; it should be relatable a word that brings the context of **awkward**.

Let us understand the meanings of the option words.

(A) gauche – unsophisticated and awkward

(B) chipper – cheerful and lively

(C) suave – charming confident and elegant

(D) adept – very skilled and proficient at something

(E) inept – having or showing no skill

(F) debonair – confident, charming and stylish

The correct answers would be 'gauche' and 'inept', both of these words bring in a negative undertone in context and mean 'socially awkward'. The words 'chipper', 'suave', 'adept' and 'debonair' bring in a positive undertone and are opposites of what the context requires.

The correct answers are A & E.

87. Let us understand the meaning of the sentence from the partial information.

It states that Guy Fawkes' actions were considered **something** when he was alive, but after his death he was called a hero. The **hint-phrase** here is '**hero and a revolutionary**'. This when combined with the signal phrase **although** suggests that during his time his actions were perceived unheroic. The word **unheroic** can be used as the **fill-in**.

Let us pre-empt the **fill-in**; it should be relatable a word that brings the context of **unheroic**.

Let us understand the meanings of the option words.

(A) benevolent – well meaning and kind

(B) nefarious – wicked or criminal

(C) reprehensible – deserving censure or condemnation

(D) salubrious – health-giving; healthy

(E) sincere – free from pretense or deceit

(F) jocular – characterized by joking; humorous or playful

The correct answers would be 'nefarious' and 'reprehensible, since only these words are closest in meaning to the word 'unheroic'. The words 'benevolent', 'salubrious', 'sincere' and 'jocular' have a positive undertone and therefore do not match the context of the sentence.

The correct answers are B & C.

88. Let us understand the meaning of the sentence from the partial information.

It states that although the common perception is that a promotion **does something** to a raise in salary, many professionals get a promotion without getting a raise in the salary. The **hint-phrase** here is '**many professionals take on a bigger title.... without a commensurate increase in compensation**'. The signal words **Even though** suggests that the expected scenario in the first half of the sentence does not follow all the time. The phrase '**results in**' can act as the **fill-in**.

Let us pre-empt the **fill-in**; it should be relatable a word that brings the context of **results in**.

Let us understand the meanings of the option words.

(A) jeopardizes – puts in situation in which there is danger of loss, harm or failure

(B) obviates – avoids or prevents

(C) entails – involves as necessary or inevitable consequence

(D) procrastinates – delays or postpones action

(E) engenders – causes or gives rise to

(F) circumvents – finds a way around

The correct answers would be 'entails' and 'engenders'. The words 'jeopardizes' is opposite to what the sentence requires. The words 'obviates' and 'circumvents' suggest 'avoiding' and this does not match the context of the sentence. Similarly, the word 'procrastinates', though means to 'result in something', and brings the context of 'delay', which is not supported by the context of the sentence.

The correct answers are C & E.

89.   Let us understand the meaning of the sentence from the partial information.

It describes Henry III's dreams and suggests that they were **something**. The **hint-phrases** here are '**dreams of autocracy**', '**in a century of constitutional ideas**', '**earned the contempt**' and '**the instability of his purpose**'. These suggest that his dreams were old-fashioned & flimsy and we also realize that people had a negative perception towards it. The word **old-fashioned** or **flimsy** can work as the **fill-in**.

Let us pre-empt the **fill-in**; it should be relatable a word that brings the context of **old fashioned** or **flimsy**.

Let us understand the meanings of the option words.

(A) anachronistic – out of its proper or chronological order, especially a person or practice that belongs to an earlier time

(B) avant-garde – favoring or introducing new and experimental ideas and methods

(C) egalitarian – based on the principle that all people are equal and deserve equal rights and opportunities

(D) antiquated – old fashioned or outdated

(E) visionary – thinking about or planning the future with imagination or wisdom

(F) populist – relating to a person who supports or seeks to appeal to the concerns of ordinary people

The correct answers would be 'anachronistic' and 'antiquated' since these are the only words that bring the context of something 'not being appropriate for the current times'; they also bring in a negative undertone that is required by the context of the sentence. The words 'avant- grade' and 'visionary' cannot fit the context of the sentence since they have a positive undertone. The words 'egalitarian' and 'populist' are opposite in meaning to the word 'autocratic' and therefore cannot describe people's perceptions of Henry's dreams.

The correct answers are A & D.

90.   Let us understand the meaning of the sentence from the partial information.

It states that the survey pilots must fly through a **particular** kind of weather and winds. The **hint** exists in context. The phrase '**maintaining their target altitude and ground**

speed, sometimes through" suggests that they must maintain complete control even when conditions get unpredictable. **Unpredictable** can therefore be the **fill-in** word.

Let us pre-empt the **fill-in**; it should be relatable a word that brings the context of **unpredictable**.

Let us understand the meanings of the option words.

(A) fickle – quickly changing

(B) clement – mild

(C) trivial – of little value or importance

(D) inconsequential – not important or significant

(E) mercurial – subject to sudden and unpredictable changes

(F) serene – calm peaceful and untroubled

The correct answers would be 'fickle' and 'mercurial'. The words 'clement' and 'serene' are contrary to what the context of the sentence requires. The words 'trivial' and 'inconsequential' aren't relevant to what the sentence requires.

The correct answers are A & E.

91. Let us understand the meaning of the sentence from the partial information.

It states that the Bulgarians publicly attacked the Servians describing them as **something** and faithless. The **hint-words** here are '**denounced**' and '**faithless**'. These suggest that we need a word with a negative undertone. Since the only information provided by the sentence is that something negative was said about the Servians, let us look at the options, and eliminate answers that don't fit the context or the fit the tone.

Let us understand the meanings of the option words.

(A) perfidious – deceitful and untrustworthy

(B) laconic – using very few words

(C) solemn – formal and dignified

(D) terse – sparing in the use of words

(E) craven – contemptibly lacking in courage; cowardly

(F) austere – severe and strict in manner or attitude

The correct answers would be 'perfidious' and 'craven', since only these words bring in a negative undertone that is relevant to the context of this sentence. The words 'laconic' and 'terse' mean to use 'only a few words': this does not fit the context of the sentence. The words 'solemn' and 'austere' sound a bit negative but in context they would portray a positive quality and are therefore not relevant.

The correct answers are A & E.

92. Let us understand the meaning of the sentence from the partial information.

It states that Jeff made an ill-considered remark about AIDS and apologized for it stating that it is terribly easy to be **something** about an epidemic that one has never witnessed firsthand. The **hint-word** here is **frivolous**. The fact that he apologized and explains his actions would suggest that it is easy to be casual. The word **casual** can therefore act as the **fill-in**.

Let us pre-empt the **fill-in**; it should be relatable a word that brings the context of **casual**.

Let us understand the meanings of the option words.

(A) colloquial – using familiar or ordinary conversation

(B) cognizant – having knowledge or awareness of something

(C) cavalier – lacking proper concern; offhand

(D) tangential – diverting from a particular course; erratic

(E) tactful – having or showing skill and sensitivity in dealing with others or with difficult issues

(F) offhand – without previous thought or consideration; offensive

The correct answers would be 'cavalier' and 'offhand' since only these words bring in the context of being 'unserious' or 'causal' in a negative light. The words 'colloquial' and 'cognizant' do not carry a negative undertone and therefore do not fit the context of the sentence. 'Tangential' might fit the context of the sentence but on close evaluation it is not the best fit with the **hint-word** 'frivolous' and is therefore not relevant to the context of the sentence. The word 'tactful' is in contrast with what the context of the sentence requires.

The correct answers are C & F.

93. Let us understand the meaning of the sentence from the partial information.

It states that Taylor criticized people who participate in a particular trend, but that she saves her greatest disrespect and **something** for American celebrities who do the same. The **hint-word** here is **scorn**. The context suggests that she looks down on people who follow the trend but does not echo the same about celebrities who do that same. The phrase '**harsh criticism**' can work as the **fill-in**.

Let us pre-empt the **fill-in**; it should be relatable a word that brings the context of **harsh criticism**.

Let us understand the meanings of the option words.

(A) opprobrium – harsh criticism or censure

(B) obloquy – strong public condemnation

(C) blandishments – flattery; cajolery

(D) piety – the quality of being religious or reverent

(E) plaudits – the applause of an audience; praise

(F) priggishness – self-righteous superiority

The correct answers would be 'opprobrium' and 'obloquy' since they both bring in the context of 'harsh criticism'. The words 'priggishness' does not match the required context of 'criticism'. The words 'blandishment', 'piety' and 'plaudits' are all positive words that are opposite to what the sentence requires.

The correct answers are A & B.

94. Let us understand the meaning of the sentence from the partial information.

It states that Peter shared some jokes, which addressed certain bizarre practices people of a community follow; however at the end, they took a/an **some** turn that left the audience feeling uncomfortable and disturbed. The **hint-phrase** is '**leaving the audience disconcerted and fazed**'. Since the audience who was laughing at jokes, but suddenly felt uncomfortable and disturbed, it implies that at the end, Peter may have pushed his jokes too far, making people uncomfortable.

Let us pre-empt the **fill-in**; it should be a relatable word that brings the context of **discomfiting**.

Let us understand the meanings of the option words.

(A) edifying – moralizing; expressing one's disapproval of something

(B) squeamish – cowardly; hysterical

(C) woozy – unsteady; lightheaded

(D) preachy – giving moral advice in a tedious or self-righteous way

(E) soothing – gentle; comforting

(F) uncanny – weird; mysterious

The correct answers would be 'edifying' and 'preachy', both of these words bring in a when used in context suggests a tone that will make an audience uncomfortable because they might feel judged or victimized. While 'woozy' and 'soothing' will rather do the opposite of what the audience would do, 'squeamish' and 'uncanny' are not relevant to the context of 'making someone feel uncomfortable'.

The correct answers are A & D.

95. Let us understand the meaning of the sentence from the partial information.

It states that the captain's decision of including five bowlers paid off as expected. His next move was to take advantage of his assets (bowlers) to **do something** about his decision. The **hint-phrase** here is '**yielded results**'. With the use of signal punctuation ; (semi-colon), we infer that following thought must be in the same direction. The captain must **substantiate** his unpopular decision to capitalize on the availability of five bowlers.

Let us pre-empt the **fill-in**; it should be a relatable word that brings the context of **substantiate**.

Let us understand the meanings of the option words.

(A) corroborate – validate; uphold

(B) contravene – breach; flout

(C) abjure – repudiate; deny

(D) plough – turn up the earth of (an area of land) with a plough, especially before sowing

(E) upbear – sustain; support

(F) burlesque – lampoon; mock

The correct answers would be 'corroborate' and 'upbear', both of these words bring in a meaning that is in line with the pre-empted word 'substantiate'. While 'contravene', 'abjure' and 'burlesque' are opposite of what the **fill-in** suits, 'plough' is awkward to use in this context.

The correct answers are A & E.

96. Let us understand the meaning of the sentence from the partial information.

It described the troubled relationship between North Korea and South Korea. The ties between them are **something** enough that despite external intervention may lead to disaster. The **hint-phrase** is '**it may lead to cataclysm**'. **Troubled** or **cataclysmic** can be best suited for the **fill-in**.

Let us pre-empt the **fill-in**; it should be a relatable a word that brings the context of **troubled**.

Let us understand the meanings of the option words.

(A) quixotic – idealistic; romantic; dreamy

(B) turbulent – violent; unstable

(C) volatile – unpredictable; turbulent

(D) superfluous – surplus; excessive

(E) pecuniary – financial; economic

(F) inundated – overwhelmed; filled

The correct answers would be 'turbulent' and 'volatile', both of these words bring in a meaning that is in line with pre-empt word 'troubled'. The words 'superfluous', 'inundated', 'quixotic' and 'pecuniary' do not bring in the context of 'troubled' or 'cataclysmic' and are therefore not in line with what the sentence requires.

The correct answers are B & C.

97. Let us understand the meaning of the sentence from the partial information.

It states that James Bonds' persistent success to **do something with** opponents' hideouts has inspired many movie-makers to make similar movies. The word "**sabotage**" acts as the **hint-phrase**. The word **thwart** or **sneak in** could act as the fill-in.

Let us pre-empt the **fill-in**; it should be a relatable word that brings the context of **destroy** or **sneak in**.

Let us understand the meanings of the option words.

(A) estrange – alienate; dissatisfy

(B) foil – stop; thwart; halt

(C) intrude – infringe; encroach; trespass

(D) invade – raid; enter; assault

(E) flinch – start; cringe; shudder

(F) inundate – overwhelm; flood

The correct answers would be 'intrude' and 'invade'. While 'foil' is vaguely related, it is not correct since James Bond would 'thwart the plans' of the opponent but cannot technically thwart the secret hideout. The words 'estrange' and 'flinch' are not relevant to the required context of the sentence.

The correct answers are C & D.

98. Let us understand the meaning of the sentence from the partial information.

It states that corruption is not yet won over or eradicated, it has rather been **something** for a while. Further it states that after the election, it will be widespread as was before. The usage of **signal word** '**hardly**' implies that the current state of corruption is opposite to that of being 'surmounted'. With the use of **hint words: surmounted** and **rampant**, we can infer that the **fill-in** could be **dormant**.

Let us pre-empt the **fill-in**; it should be a relatable word that brings the context of **dormant**.

Let us understand the meanings of the option words.

(A) languished – failed; waste away; ailed

(B) crippled – disable; impair; weaken

(C) stagnant – still; stationary; quiet

(D) escalating – intensifying; rising; mounting

(E) quiescent – inactive; inoperative

(F) regurgitating – repeating; rehearsing; spewing up

The correct answers would be 'stagnant' and 'quiescent'. While 'languished' and 'crippled' bring in the meaning of 'weakened', they are incorrect. This is a good question to understand the tone of the author. We can infer that the corruption is talked about in a negative sense, and anticipating that '**corruption is crippled or languished for a while**' is illogical. The word 'escalating' is opposite to what the sentence requires. The word 'regurgitating' is irrelevant in context.

The correct answers are C & E.

99. Let us understand the meaning of the sentence from the partial information.

It states that though George appears **something**, his demonstration of apparently mystical wisdom received smirking (negative) responses from the grade students. With the use of signal word 'though', we can infer that the following thought would go in the opposite direction. **hint-phrase 'seemingly uncanny wisdom'** and '**received grimacing responses**' suggest that the **fill-in** must be something **knowledgeable**.

Let us pre-empt the **fill-in**; it should be a relatable word that brings the context of **knowledgeable**.

Let us understand the meanings of the option words.

(A) tyro – novice; beginner

(B) neophyte – novice; beginner

(C) greenhorn – novice; beginner

(D)   rustic – pastoral; rural

(E)   dexterous – expert; deft

(F)   adroit – expert; deft

The correct answers would be 'dexterous' and 'adroit'. While 'tyro', 'neophyte', and 'greenhorn' are antonyms of what the fill-in requires, 'rustic' is not relevant in the context.

The correct answers are E & F.

100.   Let us understand the meaning of the sentence from the partial information.

It states that for a person from Western part of the world, the difference between two formats of Cricket sport is trifling (nominal), but it is of **something** for a person of the sub-continent regions. With the use of **signal word** '**Though**' and **hint-phrase** '**difference .... is trifling**', we can infer that the **fill-in** must be antonym of trifling (nominal); **very important** can be a good choice for the **fill-in**.

Let us pre-empt the **fill-in**; it should be a relatable word that brings the context of **very important**.

Let us understand the meanings of the option words.

(A)   synoptic – summary; short version

(B)   null and void – nothing; of no significance

(C)   crucial – important; vital; essential

(D)   immense – huge; vast

(E)   optional – voluntary; discretionary

(F)   nominal – minor; small

The correct answers would be 'crucial' and 'immense'. While 'null and void', 'nominal' are antonyms of what the fill-in requires, 'synoptic' and 'optional' are not relevant in the context.

The correct answers are C & D.

Chapter 7

Text Completion – Solutions

1-blank TC questions

1. Let us understand the meaning of the sentence from partial information.

    It states that in America turkey is the most popular food whereas in Europe Danish meatballs are not the most popular but evenly **something** among a few varied foods. The later part of the sentence provides the **hint** for the **fill-in**. **Something** is a characteristic that describes that Danish meatballs share their popularity with other equally popular dishes. **Shared** can act a good **fill-in**.

    Let us pre-empt the **fill-in**; it should be a relatable word from the synonym family of **shared**.

    Let us understand the meanings of the option words.

    (A) distributed – given or shared of a unit of (something) to each of a number of recipients

    (B) qualified – limited or restricted; fitted for a particular position or office

    (C) viewed – regarded with a particular attitude; looked at

    (D) influenced – inspired; guided

    (E) noted – well known; famous

    The correct answer would be 'distributed'. 'Influenced', 'viewed 'and 'noted' do not show the shared character of popularity. 'Qualified' would be irrelevant to what is said in the sentence.

    The correct answer is A.

2. Let us understand the meaning of the sentence from partial information.

    It states that the neuroscientist thinks that our journals and videos are a way of mass **something**. The later part of the sentence provides the **hint** for the **fill-in**. **Something** is a characteristic that describes that currently people have false beliefs and only a stroke of luck will equip us with required knowledge to reproduce a new organ. **Misunderstanding** can act as a good **fill-in**.

    Let us pre-empt the **fill-in**; it should be a relatable word from the synonym family of **misunderstanding**.

    Let us understand the meanings of the option words.

    (A) insanity – the state of being seriously mentally ill; madness

    (B) newness – the state or quality of being new; novel or unused

    (C) hallucination – an illusion; a distortion of a real external stimulus

    (D) frenzy – a temporary madness; hysteria

    (E) cataclysm – a momentous and violent event marked by overwhelming upheaval and demolition

    The correct answer would be 'hallucination'. While 'Insanity', and 'frenzy' are extreme and do not show that the people have mass 'misunderstanding', 'cataclysm' is not relevant to the context. 'Newness' is not correct according to what is said in the sentence.

    The correct answer is C.

3. Let us understand the meaning of the sentence from the partial information.

It states that according to a research done in 1980, the probability of using mobile phones was thought to be almost unlikely: this is suggested to be a **something** in today's perspective. There is no specific **hint-word** in this sentence. Yet, the entire sentence gives a context of what the blank requires. The word **foolish** or **unbelievable** could work in this context since we know that the use mobile phones is quite rampant and an assumption that assumes its impossibility would sound quite stupid.

Let us pre-empt the **fill-in**; it should be a relatable word that brings the context of **unbelievable** or **foolish**.

Let us understand the meanings of the option words.

(A) nescient – lacking knowledge; ignorant

(B) succinct – clearly expressive in few words; concise

(C) indolent – a disposition to avoid exertion; slothful

(D) outmoded – antiquated; old fashioned

(E) incredulous – dubious; outrageous

The correct answer is 'incredulous' since this agrees with the meaning of 'unbelievable' in context. The word 'succinct' is opposite of what the context requires. The word 'outmoded' though seeming relevant doesn't bring in the level of negativity that the context required, since 'outmoded' only means to be old fashioned or antiquated. The words 'nescient' and 'indolent' do not match the context of the sentence.

The correct answer is E.

4. Let us understand the meaning of the sentence from the partial information.

It states that Da Vinci was famous for his art but his novel designs while understated had a more **particular** kind of impact as it influenced design of aircrafts centuries into the future. The hint-phrase here is '**its principles strongly influenced aircraft design well into the 21nd century**'. The word **long lasting** could act as the **fill-in**.

Let us pre-empt the **fill-in**; it should be a relatable word that brings the context of **long lasting**.

Let us understand the meanings of the option words.

(A) indelible – permanent; enduring

(B) laudatory – expressing praise; complimenting

(C) ephemeral – lasting a very short time; temporary

(D) indigent – lacking food, clothing and other necessities; needy

(E) filial – befitting a son or daughter

The correct answer is 'indelible' since this agrees with the meaning of 'long lasting'. The word 'ephemeral' is opposite of what the context requires. The words 'laudatory', 'indigent' and 'filial' are not relevant to the context of the sentence.

The correct answer is A.

5. Let us understand the meaning of the sentence from the partial information.

It states that the scientist makes an effort to remain **something** with the newest research in his field even though he is retired. The only **hint** here is contextual and the word **'retired'**. With the presence of the **signal word 'Though'**, we can infer that the following thought would be in contrast to what is stated; the phrase remain **'in touch with'** can work as the **fill-in**.

Let us pre-empt the **fill-in**; it should be a relatable word/phrase that brings the context of **in touch with**.

Let us understand the meanings of the option words.

(A) enchanted by – under a cast of a spell; attracted

(B) astounded by – bewildered; astonished

(C) cognizant of – fully informed; aware

(D) apathetic to – showing lack of concern or interest; being indifferent

(E) taken aback by – surprised at something unexpected; confused

The correct answer is 'cognizant of' since this matches the context of 'keep in touch' with newest research. The words 'enchanted by', 'astounded by' and 'taken aback by' bring in a meaning of being surprised by something: this cannot be achieved by 'making an effort' and cannot make sense in context. The word 'apathetic to' is opposite of what the sentence requires.

The correct answer is C.

6. Let us understand the meaning of the sentence from the partial information.

It states that January's Tsunami was but a **something** to the coming year. We know that the rest of the year was followed by similar (or even worse) natural and economic disasters. The **hint** here is contextual since we know that the Tsunami happened in the beginning of the year and a lot more disasters followed the rest of the year – the word **'introduction'** or **'beginning'** could work as the **fill-in**.

Let us pre-empt the **fill-in**; it should be a relatable word that brings the context of **beginning**.

Let us understand the meanings of the option words.

(A) expurgation – amendment by removing words deemed offensive; clean

(B) prelude – an action or event serving as an introduction to something

(C) orgy – celebration in a wild or drunken way

(D) prolegomenon – a discussion in the preliminary stage; an introduction

(E) monologue – a prolonged talk by a single person

The correct answer is 'prelude' since this matches the context of 'beginning' or 'introduction'. The words 'expurgation', 'orgy' and 'monologue' do not fit the context of the sentence. The word 'prolegomenon' is an introduction used only in the context of a literary piece and therefore cannot fit the required context.

The correct answer is B.

7. Let us understand the meaning of the sentence from the partial information.

It states that after the disagreement that lasted for a short time, the group chose a leader and did **something** into a harmonious group. The contextual hint here is that the **fill-in** will contrast the **hint-phrase 'squabble'**. The word **'formed'** can act as the **fill-in**.

Let us pre-empt the **fill-in**; it should be a relatable word that brings the context of **formed**.

Let us understand the meanings of the option words.

(A) collocated – set or placed together; set side by side

(B) mangled – injured severely or disfigured; spoiled or ruined

(C) shriveled – contracted or wrinkled; become useless

(D) commingled – mixed or mingled together; combined

(E) appropriated – take (something) for one's own use, typically without the owner's permission

The correct answer is 'commingled'. The words 'collocated' does not fit the context since this means to be placed next to one another and does not bring in the context of 'formed'. The words 'mangled' and 'shriveled' are in contrast to what the context requires. The word 'appropriated' is not relevant to the context of the sentence.

The correct answer is D.

8. Let us understand the meaning of the sentence from the partial information.

It states that the writer added **something** into the movie: the **hint-phrases** here are **'set in the 16ⁿᵈ century'** and **'used a calculator'**. These suggest that there were inconsistencies in the chronological correctness of certain objects. The word **'inconsistencies'** can work as the fill-in.

Let us pre-empt the **fill-in**; it should be a relatable word that brings the context of **inconsistencies**.

Let us understand the meanings of the option words.

(A) vapidity – lacking life or sharpness; boring or dull

(B) shibboleth – a slogan or catchword; a common saying with little truth in it

(C) rigmarole – an elaborate procedure; foolish talk

(D) metachronism – occurring at a different time than a similar event

(E) inferences – a logical conclusion

The correct answer is 'metachronis' since this is closest in meaning to 'inconsistencies in time'. The words 'shibboleth', 'rigmarole' and 'inferences' do not fit the context of the sentence. The word 'vapidity' is very negative and goes beyond the scope of the context.

The correct answer is D.

9. Let us understand the meaning of the sentence from the partial information.

It describes Chavez. The sentence illustrates how Chavez has done inhumane things and is a power hungry tyrant, yet he came off as surprisingly **something** in his interview. The phrase **'could explain why such reprehensible rulers are able to gain the loyalties of**

so many of their subjects' is the **hint-phrase** in the sentence. Therefore he must have come off as very **pleasant** and **charming** in the interview.

Let us pre-empt the **fill-in**; it should be a relatable word that brings the context of '**pleasant**'.

Let us understand the meanings of the option words.

(A)   magnanimous – generous or forgiving

(B)   malignant – evil in nature

(C)   austere – severe or strict in manner and attitude

(D)   draconian – excessively harsh and severe

(E)   grandiose – extravagantly or pretentiously imposing in appearance or style

The correct answer is 'magnanimous'. Even though 'magnanimous' does not mean 'pleasant', it is the only word with a positive undertone and in context could explain why people might find him trustworthy. The words 'malignant', 'austere' and 'draconian' are opposites of what the sentence requires. The word 'grandiose' is not relevant to the context of the sentence.

The correct answer is A.

10.   Let us understand the meaning of the sentence from the partial information.

It states that much of the perceptions about the Columbine incident are wrong since it is rooted in myth, run by bad news outlets with rumor and **something**. The **fill-in** must relate to the overall idea of 'having no real proof'. The word '**guesswork**' could act as the **fill-in**.

Let us pre-empt the **fill-in**; it should be a relatable word that brings the context of '**guesswork**'.

Let us understand the meanings of the option words.

(A)   serendipity – the occurrence and development of events by chance in a happy or beneficial way

(B)   solace – feeling of comfort

(C)   certitude – absolute certainty or conviction that something is the case

(D)   conjecture – an opinion or conclusion formed on the basis of incomplete information

(E)   iniquity – immoral or grossly unfair behavior

The correct answer is 'conjecture', since this goes with the word 'guesswork'. The word 'certitude' and 'solace' are opposite of what the sentence requires. The words 'serendipity' and 'iniquity' are not relevant to the context of 'guesswork'.

The correct answer is D.

11.   Let us understand the meaning of the sentence from the partial information.

It states that students famous in school end up not being as famous as adults. The **hint-phrase** in the sentence is '**relative obscurity**'. The phrase '**pushed down to**' can work as the **fill-in**.

Let us pre-empt the **fill-in;** it should be a relatable word that brings the context of **'pushed down to'**.

Let us understand the meanings of the option words.

(A) spent on – left with no energy

(B) satiated with – satisfied to the fullest with

(C) regaled with – entertained or amused with

(D) relegated to – assigned to an inferior rank or position

(E) pacified with – quelled the agitation or anger with

The correct answer is 'relegated to' since this brings the context of 'pushed down to'. The words 'spent on', 'satiated with', 'regaled with' and 'pacified with' are all contrary to the context the sentence requires.

The correct answer is D.

12. Let us understand the meaning of the sentence from the partial information.

It describes what biologists do to pre-Darwinian theories. The **hint-phrase 'tend to eliminate rather than revise'** suggests that these scientists are thereby **rejecting** the older theories' uniqueness and existence.

Let us pre-empt the **fill-in;** it should be a relatable word that brings the context of **'rejecting'**.

Let us understand the meanings of the option words.

(A) contesting – opposing as mistaken or wrong

(B) extolling – praising enthusiastically

(C) explaining – making something clear by describing it in more detail

(D) transfiguring – transforming into something more beautiful or elevated

(E) anticipating – guessing or being aware of (what will happen) and taking action in order to be prepared

The correct answer is 'contesting'. The words 'extolling' and 'transfiguring' have a positive undertone and are therefore opposites of what the sentence requires. The words 'explaining' and 'anticipating' do not logically follow the context of 'rejecting'.

The correct answer is A.

13. Let us understand the meaning of the sentence from the partial information.

It states that Russian officials and television networks have portrayed the revolutionaries a fascist **something,** intent on robbing Russians of their rights. The **hint-word 'stripping ethnic Russians of their rights'** suggests that this group of people were viewed as enemies of the country. The word **'antagonistic group'** could work in context.

Let us pre-empt the **fill-in;** it should be a relatable word that brings the context of **'antagonistic group'**.

Let us understand the meanings of the option words.

(A) encomium – a speech or piece of writing that praises someone

(B) regime – a government

(C) reform – the action or process of reforming an institution or practice

(D) cabal – a secret political clique or faction

(E) leadership – the leaders of an organization or group

The correct answer is 'cabal' since only this is close to the context of an 'antagonistic group'. The words 'encomium' is not relevant to the context of the sentence. The words 'regime', 'reform' and 'leadership' bring in a context that does not agree with what the sentence requires.

The correct answer is D.

14. Let us understand the meaning of the sentence from the partial information.

    It states that although archaeologists are always portrayed digging for artefacts in the desert, they actually spend a lot of time in the libraries doing research. The phrase '**most of their research actually happens in the libraries**' is the **hint-phrase**. The word '**made possible**' can act as the **fill-in**.

    Let us pre-empt the **fill-in;** it should be a relatable word that brings the context of '**made possible**'.

    Let us understand the meanings of the option words.

    (A) emblazoned – conspicuously inscribe or display a design on

    (B) perused – read (something), typically in a thorough or careful way

    (C) absconded – left hurriedly and secretly, typically to escape from custody or avoid arrest

    (D) incited – encouraged or stirred up

    (E) circumscribed – restricted within limits

    The correct answer is 'incited' as this brings the context of 'made possible'. The word 'circumscribed' is opposite of what the context requires. The words 'emblazoned', 'perused' and 'absconded' are not relevant to the context of the sentence.

    The correct answer is D.

15. Let us understand the meaning of the sentence from the partial information.

    It states that Bernie comes off as **something** rather than eloquent since his speeches are too many long and bombastic. The hint-phrase here is 'rather than eloquent'. The sentence therefore suggests that he comes off as **showy** or **pretentious**.

    Let us pre-empt the **fill-in;** it should be a relatable word that brings the context of '**showy**' or '**pretentious**'.

    Let us understand the meanings of the option words.

    (A) glib – fluent but insincere and shallow

    (B) fatuous – silly and pointless

    (C) loquacious – tending to talk a great deal

    (D) unscrupulous – having or showing no moral principles

(E) taciturn – reserved or uncommunicative in speech; saying little

The correct answer is 'glib' since this brings in the context of being 'showy' and 'pretentious'. The word 'taciturn' is opposite of what the context suggests. The word 'loquacious' may be true but the sentence only suggests that his speeches are 'showy' and not that they are only 'long' or 'lengthy'. The words 'fatuous' and 'unscrupulous' are very negative and there is no information in the sentence that supports either of these words.

The correct answer is A.

16. Let us understand the meaning of the sentence from the partial information.

It states that the writer of the book **does something** to those who stick to a single employer for the entire of their careers. The **hint-phrase** '**almost all competent workers change jobs at least once every three years**' suggests that he feels those who stay with one employer are not competent. Therefore he probably **scolds** or **insults**.

Let us pre-empt the **fill-in;** it should be a relatable word that brings the context of '**scolds**' or '**insults**'.

Let us understand the meanings of the option words.

(A) chides – scolds or rebukes

(B) approbates – approves formally

(C) immolates – kills or offers as a sacrifice especially through burning

(D) placates – makes less angry or hostile

(E) censors – examines (a book, film, etc.) officially and suppress unacceptable parts

The correct answer is 'chides'. The words 'approbates' and 'placates' are opposites of what the sentence requires. The words 'immolates' and 'censors' do not make sense in the context of this sentence.

The correct answer is A.

17. Let us understand the meaning of the sentence from the partial information.

It states that students complained that the professor gave out **some kind** of criticism and therefore the management asked him to be more diplomatic. The **hint-phrase** '**adhere to a more diplomatic approach**' suggests that he was not diplomatic before. The word '**harsh**' could work in context.

Let us pre-empt the **fill-in;** it should be a relatable word that brings the context of '**harsh**'.

Let us understand the meanings of the option words.

(A) nondescript – lacking distinctive or interesting features or characteristics

(B) scathing – witheringly scornful; severely critical

(C) insipid – lacking flavor; weak or tasteless

(D) subtle – so delicate or precise as to be difficult to analyze or describe

(E) judicious – having, showing, or done with good judgment or sense

The correct answer is 'scathing'. The words 'nondescript', 'insipid' and 'subtle' bring the context of lacking intensity or flavor – this is opposite to what the context of the sentence requires. The word 'judicious' is opposite of what the sentence requires.

The correct answer is B.

18. Let us understand the meaning of the sentence from the partial information.

It states that the economic crisis has created a particular kind of job market. The **hit-phrase 'few available jobs'** suggests that the job market isn't really healthy. Therefore, **unhealthy** or **weak** could work as a **fill-in.**

Let us pre-empt the **fill-in**, it should be a relatable word that brings the context of **unhealthy** or **weak.**

Let us understand the meanings of the option words.

(A)   salubrious – health-giving; healthy

(B)   decadent – characterized by or reflecting a state of moral or cultural decline

(C)   anemic – lacking in spirit or vitality

(D)   facile – easily achieved

(E)   malignant – evil in nature or effect; malevolent

The correct answer is 'anemic' since this brings the context of 'unhealthy' or 'weak'. The word 'salubrious' is opposite of what the sentence requires. The word 'decadent' brings in the context of 'moral degradation', which doesn't fit the context of this sentence. The word 'malignant' brings in a context of 'evil natured' that is also not supported by the sentence. The word 'facile' is not relevant to the context of the sentence.

The correct answer is C.

19. Let us understand the meaning of the sentence from the partial information.

It states that in ancient Greece, young men sought out philosophical mentors, but when they didn't seek out mentors and a guru tried to guide these men it came off as patronizing (condescending) and **something**. The only **hint-word** available here is '**patronizing**'. We therefore need a negative word that is in line with **condescending**.

Let us pre-empt the **fill-in**, it should be a relatable word that brings the context of **condescending**

Let us understand the meanings of the option words.

(A)   affable – friendly, good-natured, or easy to talk to

(B)   pastoral – associated with country life

(C)   sententious – given to moralizing in a pompous or affected manner

(D)   torrential – flowing rapidly and with force

(E)   salubrious – health-giving; healthy

The correct answer is 'sententious' since this agrees with the meaning of 'condescending' and 'patronizing' in context. The word 'affable' is opposite of what the context requires. The word 'pastoral', 'torrential' and 'salubrious' are not relevant to the context of the sentence.

The correct answer is C.

20. Let us understand the meaning of the sentence from the partial information.

It describes **some people** who always tend to look at things differently than others. From context, we realize that the entire sentence provides **hints** about who these people are. The word **'unconventional thinkers'** could work in context.

Let us pre-empt the **fill-in**, it should be a relatable word that brings the context of **'unconventional thinkers'**.

Let us understand the meanings of the option words.

(A) idolaters – people who worship idols

(B) initiates – people who have been initiated into an organization or activity; newcomer

(C) sociopaths – people with a personality disorder manifesting itself in extreme anti-social attitudes and behavior

(D) mavericks – unorthodox or independent-minded person

(E) mendicants – beggars

The correct answer is 'mavericks' as this goes with the 'unconventional thinkers'. The words 'initiates' is sort of opposite of what the sentence requires since it brings in the possible context of 'inexperience'. The word 'idolaters', 'sociopaths' and 'mendicants' are not relevant to the context of the sentence.

The correct answer is D.

21. Let us understand the meaning of the sentence from the partial information.

It states that Macintyre writes about spies so craftily and so in a **particular** way that you might suspect that he himself is a spy. The **hint-words 'craftily'** and the **hint-phrase 'half suspect him of being some type of spook himself'** suggest that he wrote very **convincingly** or **vividly**.

Let us pre-empt the **fill-in**, it should be a relatable word that brings the context of **convincingly** or **vividly**.

Let us understand the meanings of the option words.

(A) tortuously – excessively lengthened or complicated

(B) surreptitiously – secretly done, especially because it would not be approved of

(C) apathetically – in a way that is showing or feeling no interest, enthusiasm, or concern

(D) ebulliently – cheerfully; enthusiastically

(E) insipidly – tastelessly

The correct answer is 'ebulliently' since this is related to 'vividly'. The words 'tortuously', 'apathetically', and 'insipidly' carry negative undertones that do not agree with what the sentence requires. The word 'surreptitiously', though a characteristic of a spy, does not make sense in this context because the author here is not writing in a surreptitious way, he is being quite expressive and vivid.

The correct answer is D.

22. Let us understand the meaning of the sentence from the partial information.

It describes and contrasts the current CEO with the pervious CEO. The **hint-phrases** here are '**The previous CEO, who was known for his aggressive tactics and hostility...**', and '**helped repair relationships**'. The **signal phrase 'in contrast'** suggests that the new CEO is quite opposite of the old CEO. The word '**friendly** makes sense in context and can work as the **fill-in**.

Let us pre-empt the **fill-in**, it should be a relatable word that brings the context of **friendly**.

Let us understand the meanings of the option words.

(A) emollient – attempting to avoid confrontation or anger; calming or conciliatory

(B) repugnant – in conflict or incompatible with

(C) sophomoric – pretentious or juvenile

(D) peripatetic – traveling from place to place, in particular working or based in various places for relatively short periods

(E) indigent – poor; needy

The correct answer is 'emollient' since this is related to 'friendly'. The words 'repugnant' is opposite of what the context requires. The word 'sophomoric' brings a negative undertone and this is not supported by the context of the sentence. The words 'peripatetic' and 'indigent' are not relevant to the context of the sentence.

The correct answer is A.

23. Let us understand the meaning of the sentence from the partial information.

It describes the subject or the interviewee. The **hint-words 'deeply unpleasant'**, '**a windy (stormy)'** and '**not particularly useful**' give us an idea of how the subject was. The word '**uncooperative**' or '**difficult to handle**' can fit the context.

Let us pre-empt the **fill-in**, it should be a relatable word that brings the context of **unco-operative**.

Let us understand the meanings of the option words.

(A) brawny – physically strong, muscular

(B) parsimonious – very unwilling to spend money or use resources

(C) laconic – using very few words

(D) fraternal – of or like a brother or brothers

(E) refractory – stubborn or unmanageable

The correct answer is 'refractory'. The words 'brawny', 'parsimonious', and 'fraternal' do not match the context of the sentence. The word 'laconic', though could be true, is not supported by the context of the sentence as it does sync with a character who is windy.

The correct answer is E.

24. Let us understand the meaning of the sentence from the partial information.

It states the biologists have indisputable evidence that suggests that life is **something** of other forms. The **hint-phrase 'no free-living creatures that live in complete solitude'** suggests that life is **'always in connection with'** other forms.

Let us pre-empt the **fill-in**, it should be a relatable word that brings the context of **'always in connection with'**.

Let us understand the meanings of the option words.

(A) isolated from – cut off from

(B) dependent on – reliant on

(C) foregrounded by – made something the most important or prominent feature

(D) antithetical to – directly opposed or contrasted to

(E) emulated by – matched or surpassed by through imitation

The correct answer is 'dependent on'. The words 'isolated from' and 'antithetical to' are opposites of what the context requires. The word 'foregrounded by' brings in a context of 'making something more prominent', but this is not supported by the context of the sentence. Likewise 'emulated by' is not supported by the context of the sentence either.

The correct answer is B.

25. Let us understand the meaning of the sentence from the partial information.

It states that although her views were contentious and sparked a lot of disagreement, people who disagreed with her rarely found fault with her expressing her views because her opinions were a **particular** way. The only **hint** here is contextual as we know that people found her views contentious and yet didn't fault her for them.

Let us evaluate the options and eliminate any unsupported options

Let us understand the meanings of the option words.

(A) reflective – relating to or characterized by deep thought; thoughtful

(B) political – motivated by a person's beliefs or actions concerning politics

(C) recondite – (of a subject or knowledge) little known; abstruse

(D) impractical– not adapted for use or action; not sensible or realistic

(E) banal – so lacking in originality as to be obvious and boring

The correct answer is 'reflective' as this brings in a positive undertone and when used in context will explain why people didn't fault her for her views. The words 'recondite', 'impractical', and 'banal' are negative in context. The word 'political' is not supported contextually by the sentence and is therefore not relevant.

The correct answer is A.

26. Let us understand the meaning of the sentence from the partial information.

It states that the evaluation team couldn't come to a unanimous agreement since the criteria of evaluation of various members of the team rested on such **some kind** of preferences. The **hint-phrase 'could not develop a consensus'** suggests that their preferences were quite different. The word **different** or **contrasting** could work in context.

Let us pre-empt the **fill-in**, it should be a relatable word that brings the context of **different**.

Let us understand the meanings of the option words.

(A) trite – lacking originality or freshness

(B) trifling – unimportant or trivial

(C) obvious – easily perceived or understood; clear, self-evident, or apparent

(D) divergent – tending to be different or develop in different directions

(E) antiquated – old-fashioned or outdated

The correct answer is 'divergent'. The words 'trite', 'trifling', 'obvious' and 'antiquated', though could be used in the sentence, do not convey the meaning of 'different' explaining why the members couldn't come to a decision.

The correct answer is D.

27. Let us understand the meaning of the sentence from the partial information.

It states that the Celina was quite different from her parents. The **hint-phrase 'parents who were known for their resolve and tranquillity…'** acted on by the **signal phrase 'in contrast to her parents'** suggest that she was quite **unpredictable** and **volatile**.

Let us pre-empt the **fill-in**, it should be a relatable word that brings the context of **volatile**.

Let us understand the meanings of the option words.

(A) placid – not easily upset or excited

(B) introverted – being shy and reticent

(C) mercurial – subject to sudden or unpredictable changes of mood or mind

(D) mendacious – not telling the truth; lying

(E) taciturn – reserved or uncommunicative in speech

The correct answer is 'mercurial'. The word 'placid' is opposite of what the sentence requires. The word 'introverted' and 'taciturn' are sort of opposites to what the sentence requires since people who are introverted and taciturn tend to not react violently and unpredictably. The word 'mendacious', though possibly true about Celina, is not something that is stated or implied by the sentence. Therefore, 'mendacious' is not supported by the context of the sentence.

The correct answer is C.

28. Let us understand the meaning of the sentence from the partial information.

It states that her essays were initially met with hostility, but even though this changed over time only a few reviewers now do **something** to her essay. The hint-word **'their opinions softened with time'** and the **signal words 'although'** and **'only a few'** suggest that although reviewers have started reacting less harshly towards her essay only a few of them actually **praise** the essays.

Let us pre-empt the **fill-in**, it should be a relatable word that brings the context of **praise.**

Let us understand the meanings of the option words.

(A)   celebrate – honor or praise publicly

(B)   revile – criticize in an abusive or angrily insulting manner

(C)   criticize – indicate the faults of (something) in a disapproving way

(D)   neglect – fail to care for properly

(E)   scrutinize – examine or inspect closely and thoroughly

The correct answer is 'celebrate'. The words 'revile', 'criticize' and 'neglect' are opposites of what the context requires. The word 'scrutinize' doesn't make sense since logically reviewers must have all scrutinized her works, the context isn't really bothered about whether the reviewers reviewed the work, or not – it's their reviews themselves that matter.

The correct answer is A.

29.   Let us understand the meaning of the sentence from the partial information.

It states that the Holy Grail puts forward **something**. The **hint-phrases** '**led powerful men for on a blind trail**' and '**no one was able to decipher**' gives us an idea about what that **something** was. The word '**impossible to solve puzzle**' could work as the **fill-in**.

Let us pre-empt the **fill-in**; it should be a relatable word that brings the context of '**impossible to solve puzzle**'.

Let us understand the meanings of the option words.

(A)   impasse – a situation from which there is no escape; deadlock

(B)   verse – a stanza; a poem

(C)   treasure – wealth or riches; valuables

(D)   commensuration – equal in amount or degree; adequate

(E)   dilemma – quandary; tight spot

The correct answer is 'impasse' since this agrees with the meaning of 'impossible to solve'. The word 'dilemma' is very close since this means 'something problematic and difficult' but this does not imply that it is 'impossible to solve or achieve'. Therefore 'impasse' is a better fit for this context. The words 'verse 'and 'commensuration' are not relevant to the context of the sentence. The word 'treasure' does not bring in the context of peril and impossibility to solve that the sentence suggests.

The correct answer is A.

30.   Let us understand the meaning of the sentence from the partial information.

It states that the book presents a simple story, but in the end it takes a **particular** turn. The **hint-phrase** '**warning people**' suggests that it takes a moralistic or lecturing turn. The word '**lecturing**' or '**moralistic**' can work as the **fill-in**.

Let us pre-empt the **fill-in**; it should be a relatable word that brings the context of '**lecturing**' or '**moralistic**'.

Let us understand the meanings of the option words.

(A)   benevolent – kind and generous; caring for others

(B)   apathetic – not having or showing emotion or interest

(C)   candid – expressing opinions or feelings in a sincere and honest way

(D)   pugnacious – ready to fight or argue; having a quarrelsome nature

(E)   sententious – expressing strong opinion about what people should and shouldn't do

The correct answer is 'sententious' as this is in line with 'lecturing'. The word 'apathetic' is incorrect in context since the book warns out of concern, which cannot stem out of apathy. The word 'benevolent' doesn't bring in the context of 'lecturing'. The word 'pugnacious' means to 'fight' this doesn't match the required context of the sentence.

The correct answer is E.

31.   Let us understand the meaning of the sentence from the partial information.

It describes the remark of the editor, he suggests that it was difficult to find the right moderator or judge for certain disagreements since nobody is **something** with regard to these issues. The **hint** here is contextual. The suggested meaning is that a fair judge of such scenarios is hard to find since such a judge will have to be completely impartial to the issues and nobody is **something** to such issues. The word '**impartial**' could work as the **fill-in**.

Let us pre-empt the **fill-in**; it should be a relatable word that brings the context of '**impartial**'.

Let us understand the meanings of the option words.

(A)   convivial – relating to good company; sociable

(B)   facetious – joking inappropriately; not serious

(C)   dispassionate – not influenced by strong emotion, and so able to be rational and impartial

(D)   equivocal – having two or more possible meanings

(E)   frivolous – silly and not serious; not important

The correct answer is 'dispassionate' as this is in line with 'impartial'. The words 'convivial', 'factious', 'equivocal' and 'frivolous' do not match the context of 'impartial' and in context they create sentences that are opposites of what is suggested.

The correct answer is C.

32.   Let us understand the meaning of the sentence from the partial information.

It states that the CEO's team members servilely praised the CEO, stating that he has never made an unwise decision. The CEO corrects this and dispels this as **something**. The phrase '**mealy-mouthed garrulity of sycophants**' acts as the **hint-phrase**. The word '**flattery**' can work as the **fill-in**.

Let us pre-empt the **fill-in**; it should be a relatable word that brings the context of '**flattery**'.

Let us understand the meanings of the option words.

(A)   treachery – betrayal of trust

(B)   impecuniousness – penniless; poverty

(C)   toadyism – flattery; sycophancy

(D)   banter – the playful and friendly exchange of teasing remarks

(E)   mimicry – the action or skill of imitating someone or something, especially in order to entertain or ridicule

The correct answer is 'toadyism' as this is in line with 'flattery' and brings in the negative undertone that the sentence requires. The word 'impecuniousness' is not relevant to the context of the sentence. The word 'treachery' thought negative does not agree with the context of 'flattery'. The word 'banter' though possible, does not completely bring the context expressed by the sentence; the context of 'flattery' is not addressed by the word 'banter'. The word 'mimicry' thought possible is not supported by the context of the sentence.

The correct answer is C.

33.   Let us understand the meaning of the sentence from the partial information.

It describes a silk dress and the mismatch between how it looks and the level of detail and intricacy involved in actually creating it. The words **'illusive modesty'** along with **'the staggering hours of hard work required to produce silk'** provides the context for the sentence and acts as the **hint-phrases**. We realize that there is a mismatch between how the silk dress looks and what actually does into creating it. Therefore, the word **'contradicts'** could work as the **fill-in**.

Let us pre-empt the **fill-in**; it should be a relatable word that brings the context of **'contradicts'**.

Let us understand the meanings of the option words.

(A)   certifies – asserts as certain; guarantees

(B)   remodels – models again; reconstructs

(C)   endows – becomes payable; furnishes with some talent

(D)   belies – fails to give a true impression of (something)

(E)   impedes – retards in movement or progress by obstacles or hindrances

The correct answer is 'belies' as this is the closest in context to 'contradicts'. The words 'certifies' and 'endows' are opposites of what the sentence requires. The word 'remodels' is not relevant to the context of the sentence. The word 'impedes' does not fit the context of the sentence.

The correct answer is D.

34.   Let us understand the meaning of the sentence from the partial information.

It describes a scenario and discusses the possible repercussions of it. That the multiplexes are shutting down, the sentence states, could cause students to return to books, as there will not be any accessible places to be **something** around in. The context of the sentence suggests that these students are wasting time in multiplexes. **'Wasting time'** can therefore act as the **fill-in**.

Let us pre-empt the **fill-in**; it should be a relatable word that brings the context of **'wasting time'**.

Let us understand the meanings of the option words.

(A)   scaling – climbing up or over (something high and steep)

(B)   loafing – spend one's time in an aimless, idle way

(C)   philandering – flirting; having multiple relationships

(D)   apportioning – dividing up and sharing

(E)   excogitating – pondering or musing

The correct answer is 'loafing' as this is the closest in context to 'wasting time'. The words 'scaling' and 'apportioning' are not relevant to the context of the sentence. The word 'excogitating' is opposite of what the sentence requires since the word carries a positive undertone. The word 'philandering' thought possible is not supported by the information provided in the sentence.

The correct answer is B.

35. Let us understand the meaning of the sentence from the partial information.

It describes a TV ad campaign strategy and the risk of using it – that using it would make the NGO look **something** rather than upright. The phrase '**rather than upright**' is the only **hint-phrase** available in the sentence. Therefore, the word '**crooked**' or '**crafty**' could act as the **fill-in**.

Let us pre-empt the **fill-in**; it should be a relatable word that brings the context of '**crooked**' or '**crafty**'.

Let us understand the meanings of the option words.

(A)   meticulous – taking extreme care about minute details; finicky

(B)   magniloquent – speaking in a lofty or grandiose style; boastful

(C)   disingenuous – lacking candor or frankness; insincere

(D)   insipid – without stimulating qualities; vapid

(E)   articulate – using language fluently; expressed with clarity

The correct answer is 'disingenuous' as this is the closest in context to 'crooked'. The words 'meticulous' and 'articulate' are opposites of what the context requires. The word 'magniloquent' does not bring in the context of being 'crafty' or 'crooked'. The word 'insipid' though negative, again doesn't being in the context of 'crafty' or 'crooked'.

The correct answer is C.

36. Let us understand the meaning of the sentence from the partial information.

It describes gun violence and how **something** it has become in the last decade. The **hint-phrase** '**that schools now mandate routine drills...**' suggests that gun violence is now so '**common**'.

Let us pre-empt the **fill-in**, it should be a relatable word that brings the context of '**common**'.

Let us understand the meanings of the option words.

(A)   ubiquitous – present, appearing, or found everywhere

(B)   perfunctory – carried out without real interest, feeling, or effort

(C)   iconoclastic – criticizing or attacking cherished beliefs or institutions

(D)   prosaic – having or using the style or diction of prose as opposed to poetry; lacking imaginativeness or originality

(E)   refulgent – shining very brightly

The correct answer is 'ubiquitous' as this fits the context of 'common' or 'something that often occurs'. The words 'perfunctory', 'iconoclastic', and 'refulgent' do not have any relevant to the context of the sentence. The word 'prosaic' brings in the context of 'ordinary,' but does not bring in the context of 'common' as something that is a common occurrence. 'Prosaic' therefore does not fit the required context of the sentence.

The correct answer is A.

37.   Let us understand the meaning of the sentence from the partial information.

It describes the perspectives of the critics regarding the book. The critics feel that the book can hardly be called **something**. The **hint-phrase** is present towards the end of the sentence: '**though the book does contain some pioneering ideas, it could hardly be called**'. Therefore, the critics thought that the book was probably unoriginal or ordinary. In other words, they must have felt that the book could hardly be called '**extraordinary**' or '**innovative**'.

Let us pre-empt the **fill-in**, it should be a relatable word that brings the context of '**innovative**'.

Let us understand the meanings of the option words.

(A)   orthodox – of the ordinary or usual type; normal

(B)   radical – characterized by departure from tradition; innovative or progressive

(C)   eccentric – unconventional and slightly strange

(D)   trivial – of little value or importance

(E)   controversial – giving rise or likely to give rise to controversy or public disagreement

The correct answer is 'radical' since this agrees with the context of 'innovative' and 'extraordinary'. The words 'orthodox' and 'trivial' are opposites of what the sentence requires. The word 'eccentric' and 'controversial' do bring in a context of being out of the ordinary. Yet these are not words with a positive undertone as does the word 'pioneering' or 'innovative', therefore, the words 'controversial' and 'eccentric' do not match the context of the sentence.

The correct answer is B.

38.   Let us understand the meaning of the sentence from the partial information.

It describes a kind of people and suggests that they earned the title of **something**. The **hint-phrases** in the sentence is '**resistance to new machines**' and '**those who try in vain to stop technological progress**'. The word '**technology haters**' could work in context.

Let us pre-empt the **fill-in**, it should be a relatable word that brings the context of **technology haters**.

Let us understand the meanings of the option words.

(A) patriarchs – the male heads of a family or tribe or institution

(B) racists – people who believe that a particular race is superior to another

(C) egalitarians – people who advocate or support the principle of equality for all people

(D) elitists – someone who has the belief that a society or system should be led by an elite

(E) luddites – persons opposed to increased industrialization or new technology

The correct answer is 'luddites', since this means to be 'afraid of and opposed to technological progress'. The words 'patriarchs' and 'racists' are not relevant to the context of the sentence. The words 'egalitarians' and 'elitists' may seem possible but will require making far-fetched assumptions to make them relatable, and since they do not share the context of 'hating technology', they can be rejected for being not relevant to the required context.

The correct answer is E.

39. Let us understand the meaning of the sentence from the partial information.

It suggests that students who are independent take care of their own needs and therefore benefit most from the **something** of constant teacher-student mentoring that other students require. The **hint-phrases** here are '**independent and self-sufficient**', '**take care of their own learning needs**' and '**which other students require**'. Therefore, in context, these independent students will benefit most from autonomy, or in other words from the **absence** of constant teacher-student mentoring. The word '**absence**' can work as the fill-in.

Let us pre-empt the **fill-in**, it should be a relatable word that brings the context of **absence**.

Let us understand the meanings of the option words.

(A) revitalization – infusion with new life and vitality

(B) legislation – process of making or enacting laws

(C) elimination – complete removal or ridding of (something)

(D) concretization – making (an idea or concept) real; giving specific or definite form to

(E) sublimation – transform (something) into a purer or idealized form

The correct answer is 'elimination' since it creates a sentence that is similar in context to that of 'absence'. The words 'revitalization', 'legislation', and 'concretization' create sentences that are in contrast with what the sentence suggests. The word 'sublimation' does not fit the context of the sentence.

The correct answer is C.

40. Let us understand the meaning of the sentence from the partial information.

It describes the scenario of inoculation development and discusses how, although the progress in this field is substantial there are still **some kind of** infant deaths each year. The **signal word** '**thought**' works with the **hint-phrase** '**advances in inoculation have been substantial**' to suggests that there are still many infant deaths each year due to diseases that can be prevented (or vaccinated against). The **fill-in** could, therefore, be **a number of**.

Let us pre-empt the **fill-in**, it should be a relatable word that brings the context of **a number of**.

Let us understand the meanings of the option words.

(A)   marginal – minor and not important; not central

(B)   fortuitous – happening by chance rather than intention

(C)   equitable – fair and impartial

(D)   significant – sufficiently great or important to be worthy of attention; noteworthy

(E)   modest – unassuming in the estimation of one's abilities or achievements

The correct answer is 'significant' as this agrees with 'a number of' and the context of 'substantial'. The words 'marginal' and 'modest' are opposites of what the sentence requires. The words 'fortuitous' and 'equitable' do not match the required context of the sentence.

The correct answer is D.

41.   Let us understand the meaning of the sentence from the partial information.

It states that as a subsequence of the recent outbreak of mad-cow disease, neighbouring countries are shifting to a more **particular** type of sampling. The words **'shift from cursory checks of farm animals to a more...'** acts as the **hint-phrase**. This suggests that they must move to a less cursory (hasty and not so thorough) inspection type. The word more **'thorough'** can work as the fill-in.

Let us pre-empt the **fill-in**, it should be a relatable word that brings the context of **thorough**.

Let us understand the meanings of the option words.

(A)   superficial – existing or occurring at or on the surface

(B)   perfunctory – carried out without real interest, feeling, or effort

(C)   rigorous – extremely thorough and careful

(D)   solicitous – characterized by or showing interest or concern

(E)   synergetic – involving interaction or cooperation of two or more agents to produce a combined effect

The correct answer is 'rigorous'. The words 'superficial' and 'perfunctory' are opposites of what the sentence requires. The word 'synergetic' suggests being productive but does not really address the context of being thorough. The word 'solicitous' does not fit the context of the sentence.

The correct answer is C.

42. Let us understand the meaning of the sentence from the partial information.

It states that the long angry (tirade) speech intended to correct a bad behaviour served only to **something** his disrespectful ways. The signal word **'ironically'** acts with the **hint-phrase 'intended to correct the insolence'** and suggests that the tirade had an effect opposite of what was intended. It therefore, served only to **amplify** his disrespectful ways.

Let us pre-empt the **fill-in**, it should be a relatable word, or a phrase that brings the context of **amplify**.

Let us understand the meanings of the option words.

(A) turn him away from – stop a certain behavior

(B) absolve him from – declare free from guilt

(C) reinforce – strengthen or support

(D) obfuscate – make obscure, unclear or unintelligible

(E) extenuate – acting in mitigation to lessen the seriousness of guilt or an offence

The correct answer is 'reinforce', since only this creates a sentence that agrees in context to the word 'amplify'. The words 'turn him away from', 'absolve him of' and 'extenuate' create sentences that are contrary to what is required by the context of the sentence. The word 'obfuscate' does not match the context of the sentence.

The correct answer is C.

43. Let us understand the meaning of the sentence from the partial information.

It describes a search for a patient who **something** from a mental health facility after assaulting staff. Based on the context of the sentence the word **'escaped'** could make sense as the **fill-in**.

Let us pre-empt the **fill-in**, it should be a relatable word that brings the context of **escaped**.

Let us understand the meanings of the option words.

(A) jettisoned – abandon or discard (someone or something that is no longer wanted)

(B) absconded – left hurriedly and secretly, typically to escape from custody or to avoid arrest

(C) arrogated – took or claimed for oneself without justification

(D) proliferated – increased rapidly in number; multiplied

(E) squabbled – noisily quarreled about something trivial

The correct answer is 'absconded', since this is closest in meaning to the context of 'escaped'. The words 'proliferated', 'squaddies' and 'arrogated' do not match the required context. The word 'jettisoned' suggests being thrown out, the context suggests that he escaped rather than being thrown out, therefore 'jettisoned' doesn't match the context of the sentence either.

The correct answer is B.

44. Let us understand the meaning of the sentence from the partial information.

It discusses the act of helping others and how it makes one feel. It also discusses how when one is sick that **something** takes on a new meaning. The **hint** in this sentence is completely contextual. We realize that the sentence is talking about '**helping others**' and this is the same concept being discussed in context of 'when you are sick'. Therefore the word '**benevolence**' could work as a fill-in.

Let us pre-empt the **fill-in**, it should be a relatable word that brings the context of '**benevolence**'.

Let us understand the meanings of the option words.

(A) infirmity – physical or mental weakness

(B) circumspection – the quality of being wary and unwilling to take risks; prudence

(C) magnanimity – the fact or condition of being magnanimous; generosity

(D) malevolence – the state or condition of being malevolent; hostility

(E) garrulity – excessive talkativeness, especially on trivial matters

The correct answer is 'magnanimity' since this brings the context of being generous and helping others. The words 'infirmity', 'circumspection', and 'garrulity' do not match the required context of the sentence. The word 'malevolence' is opposite of what the sentence requires.

The correct answer is C.

45. Let us understand the meaning of the sentence from the partial information.

It states that supporters say that biometric security is more secure because fingerprints (used in such security systems) are a/an **kind of** physical attribute. The **hint-phrase** '**can't be altered**' suggests that fingerprints stay intact or unchanging. The word '**unalterable**' could work as the **fill-in**.

Let us pre-empt the **fill-in**, it should be a relatable word that brings the context of '**unalterable**'.

Let us understand the meanings of the option words.

(A) immutable – unchanging over time or unable to be changed

(B) amorphous – without clearly defined shape or form

(C) superficial – existing or occurring at or on the surface

(D) ephemeral – lasting for a very short time

(E) picturesque – visually attractive, especially in a quaint or charming way

The correct answer is 'immutable'. The words 'amorphous' and 'ephemeral' are opposites of what the sentence requires. The words 'superficial' and 'picturesque' do not match the required context of the sentence.

The correct answer is A.

46. Let us understand the meaning of the sentence from the partial information.

It describes the artist's work and suggests that he is able to strike a **something** between the abstract and the real. The **hint-phrase** '**creating an almost surreal contrast in them**' suggests that he makes the difference between the two elements quite obvious. Therefore he strikes a **contrast** between the two. Let us reuse the **hint-word contrast** for the **fill-in**.

Let us pre-empt the **fill-in**, it should be a relatable word that brings the context of **contrast**.

Let us understand the meanings of the option words.

(A) imposture – an instance of pretending to be someone else in order to deceive others

(B) harmony – the state of being in agreement or concord

(C) dichotomy – a division or contrast between two things that are or are represented as being opposed or entirely different

(D) equipoise – balance of forces or interests

(E) serenade – a piece of music sung or played in the open air, typically by a man at night under the window of his beloved

The correct answer is 'dichotomy', since it creates a similar meaning in context to that of 'contrast'. The word 'harmony' and 'equipoise' are opposites of what the sentence requires. The word 'imposture' and 'serenade' do not match the context of the sentence.

The correct answer is C.

47. Let us understand the meaning of the sentence from the partial information.

It describes the sought after combination of traits in horses. The only **hint-phrases** are **'athleticism'** and **'successful equine competitor'**. Therefore the horse would probably require a temperament that is **'easy going'** or **'well behaved'**.

Let us pre-empt the **fill-in**, it should be a relatable word that brings the context of **'easy going'** or **'well behaved'**.

Let us understand the meanings of the option words.

(A) rancorous – characterized by bitterness or resentment

(B) dispassionate – not influenced by strong emotion, and so able to be rational and impartial

(C) nonchalant – not displaying anxiety, interest, or enthusiasm

(D) hubristic – excessive pride or self-confidence

(E) tractable – easy to control or influence

The correct answer is 'tractable' as this agrees with the context of 'well behaved' and 'easy going'. The word 'rancorous' and 'hubristic' are opposites of what the context requires. The word 'dispassionate' does not make sense in context of a horse's temperament, and is therefore not relevant in context. The word 'nonchalant' though sort of relevant in context, it takes on a negative undertone and goes against the suggested meaning of 'having an easy-going temperament'. 'Nonchalant' in context could mean to 'take things lightly' and even be 'difficult to manage'.

The correct answer is E.

48. Let us understand the meaning of the sentence from the partial information.

It states that Rick Perry did **something** to Trump's criticism. The **hint-phrase** '**Trump does not represent the Republican party**' suggests that Rick shot-down or rejected the criticism made by Trump. The word '**rejected**' could work as the **fill-in**.

Let us pre-empt the **fill-in**, it should be a relatable word that brings the context of **rejected**.

Let us understand the meanings of the option words.

(A) pacified – quelled the anger of, or excitement of

(B) anthropomorphized – attributed human characters or behavior to something

(C) eulogized – praised highly in speech or writing

(D) exsanguinated – having a person, animal, or organ drained of blood

(E) repudiated – refused to accept; rejected

The correct answer is 'repudiated', since this agrees with the context of 'rejected'. The words 'anthropomorphized' and 'exsanguinated' are not relevant to the context of the sentence. The words 'pacified' and 'eulogized', in context, create a meaning that is opposite of what the sentence suggests.

The correct answer is E.

49. Let us understand the meaning of the sentence from the partial information.

It talks about some type of people who say that they know God but act in a fashion that contradicts this. The **hint-phrase** '**but by their works they deny him, being abominable and disobedient**' suggests that they act in a **particular** way that disrespects or beings disrepute to every good work. Therefore, they are abominable and disobedient and unto every good work **disreputable**.

Let us pre-empt the **fill-in**, it should be a relatable word that brings the context of **disreputable**.

Let us understand the meanings of the option words.

(A) amicable – characterized by friendliness and absence of discord

(B) sanguine – optimistic or positive, especially during times of hardship

(C) fictitious – not real or true; fabricated

(D) reprobate – unprincipled

(E) felicitous – well-chosen or suited to the circumstances

The correct answer is 'reprobate' as this goes with 'disreputable'. The words 'amicable', 'sanguine', and 'felicitous' are opposites of what the sentence requires. The word 'fictitious' does not agree with the context of the sentence.

The correct answer is D.

50. Let us understand the meaning of the sentence from the partial information.

It describes the change in perception the world and Japan went through about rugby. The sentence says that once considered a **particular** type of sport, rugby is now popular.

The phrase '**suddenly. . . is in vogue**' suggests that it wasn't so popular before. The word '**not so mainstream**' could work in context.

Let us pre-empt the **fill-in**, it should be a relatable word that brings the context of **not so mainstream**.

Let us understand the meanings of the option words.

(A)   querulous – complaining in a rather petulant or whining manner

(B)   pompous – affectedly grand, solemn, or self-important

(C)   niche – a specialized but profitable segment of the market

(D)   commonplace – not unusual; ordinary

(E)   reprehensible – deserving censure or condemnation

The correct answer is 'niche' since this is in line with the context of 'not so mainstream'. The words 'pompous', and 'commonplace' are opposites of what the context suggests. The words 'querulous' and 'reprehensible' do not fit the suggested context of the sentence.

The correct answer is C.

2-blanks TC questions

51. Let us understand the meaning of the sentence from the partial information.

The sentence expresses scientists' guesses on non-occurrence of an anticipated outcome of animal species despite that fact that the same outcome occurred with plants.

Thus, we can infer that both the blanks are necessarily the same. These kinds of questions are either too easy or too hard; easy on a count that if you get a hint for one blank, the other follows, however if you don't, the other follows the same fate.

So, **fill-in 1** is **follow an outcome** and **fill-in 2** is **following an outcome.**

The **hint-phrase** is **once ample oxygen enveloped the Earth's surface** and **signal words – 'sooner even though'** further help to understand the **fill-ins**.

Let us pre-empt **fill-ins**.

So, the sentence essentially means that once sufficient oxygen was available and plants started growing, why animal species did not develop soon after that.

So, **fill-in 1** should be relatable words from the synonym family of **develop**, and **fill-in 2** should be relatable words from the synonym family of **developing.**

Let us understand the meanings of the option words from the blank (i).

(A) vanish – destroy; wane

(B) emblematize – serve as an emblem of; represent by an emblem

(C) burgeon – grow rapidly; prosper

The correct answer would be 'burgeon'. While 'extinct' is opposite of what we need, 'emblematize' is unrelated in the context.

Let us understand the meanings of the option words from the blank (ii).

(D) emulsifying – changing state; altering form

(E) vanishing – destroying; dying

(F) sprouting – prospering; developing

The correct answer would be 'sprouting'. While 'vanishing' is opposite of what we need, 'emulsifying' does not suit in the context. Though 'vanish' and 'vanishing' also make relatable pair, they are incorrect, as ample oxygen would defy the logic of extinction of species.

The correct answers are C & F.

52. Let us understand the meanings of the sentences from the partial information.

The sentence describes Contingency theory. The theory says that managers make decisions based on the situations at hand, which means that their decision making processes differ on situations. Second sentence starts with a **signal word** – While, which implies that the two leadership approaches are in contrast. Since there can be many leadership approaches and their knowledge is outside the scope of GRE-SE, we cannot pre-empt the **fill-ins** in this question, except that they are contrasting.

Let us understand the meanings of the option words from the blanks (i).

(A) despotic – autocratic

(B) participative – driven by contribution of all

(C) luscious – highly pleasing to the taste or smell

Option A and B are two leadership approaches, and both may qualify for the **fill-in 1**; since 'despotic' and 'participative' leadership approaches are in contrast to each other, it will depend on which goes in sync with that from **fill-in 2.**

Let us understand the meanings of the option words from the blanks (ii).

(D) transphobic – unreasoning hostility, aversion, etc., toward transgender people

(E) tyrannical – autocratic

(F) parching – to make dry, hot, or thirsty

Only option E is a leadership approach that contrasts 'participative', thus the correct answer for blank (ii) is E. Since 'tyrannical' means autocratic, the opposite of it in the blank (i) option is 'participative'.

The correct answers are B & E.

53. Let us understand the meaning of the sentence from the partial information.

The sentence describes Jemima's qualities and also describes how her colleagues perceive her. The **hint-phrase** provided here and that gives us an idea about Jemima's true nature is '**her habit of being brutally honest**'. The **fill-in 1** is a direct parallel to this and the sentence suggests that people mistake her **brutal honesty** for **something**. **Fill-in 1** can therefore be the word **brutal honesty**.

Let us understand the meanings of the option words from blank (i).

(A) torpor – mental inactivity; lethargy

(B) candor – quality of being open and honest; frankness

(C) hubris – excessive pride or self-confidence

The correct answer for blank (i) is candor. The words 'torpor' and 'hubris' do not fit the context of the sentence.

Let us pre-empt **fill-in 2**. The sentence suggests that people mistake her brutal honesty with **something**. The context of the sentence suggests that this must have a negative undertone. The word **arrogance** or **meanness** can word as the **fill-in 2**.

Let us understand the meanings of the option words from blank (ii).

(D) acrimony – bitterness or ill feeling

(E) modesty – humility; unpretentiousness

(F) complacence – feeling of smug or uncritical satisfaction with oneself or one's achievements

The correct answer for blank (ii) is 'acrimony' since this matches the context of meanness. The word 'modesty' has a positive undertone and therefore does not match the context of the sentence. The word 'complacence' though negative in context, does not bring in the meaning of arrogance or meanness that the sentence requires.

The correct answers are B & D.

54. Let us understand the meaning of the sentence from the partial information.

The sentence describes the general reactions to Sigmund Freud's work; it states that reactions since 1930 have wavered between extremes, and that more recently psychoanalysts have esteemed his work more highly. The **hint-phrase** for **fill-in 1** is '**fluctuated between adoration and something**'. This suggests that reactions ranged between praise and criticism. The word **criticism** serves as **fill-in 1**.

Let us understand the meanings of the option words from blank (i).

(4) peregrination – a long meandering journey

(5) condescension – an attitude of patronizing superiority; disdain

(6) veneration – great respect; reverence

The correct answer for blank (i) is 'condescension' since this contrasts the word 'adulation'. The words 'peregrination' is not relevant to the context of the sentence. The word 'veneration' is opposite to what the context requires.

Let us pre-empt **fill-in 2**. The sentence suggests that professionals who came after Freud esteemed his work more highly than **some people**. Through context we realize that the sentence refers to psychoanalysts from different time frames. **Fill-in 2** needs to be a word that brings in the meaning of '**people who worked at the same time**'.

Let us understand the meanings of the option words from blank (ii).

(D) progenitors – ancestors or parents

(E) archetypes – very typical examples of a certain person or thing

(F) contemporaries – people living at the same time

The word 'contemporaries' suits the context of the sentence. The words 'progenitors' and 'archetypes' do not go logically with the meaning intended in the sentence.

The correct answers are B & F.

55. Let us understand the meaning of the sentence from the partial information.

The sentence describes the works of Harold Bloom and suggests that it cannot be viewed as some **type of** creation because **something** was done by earlier poets to Harold's works. Blank (i) is easier to work with: the **hint-word** here is '**earlier poets**'; there are no other hints here. Let us work by eliminating options that cannot fit the context and do not logically agree with the **hint-word**.

Let us understand the meanings of the option words from blank (i).

(A) were inspired by – were motivated by

(B) had an influence on – had an impact on

(C) were antithetical with – were in contrast with

The phrase 'were inspired by' does not follow logically since it is impossible for earlier poets to be 'inspired' by a poet from the future. The phrases 'had an influence on' and 'were antithetical with' could both fit the context of the sentence. We need to match the options to those of blank (ii) to be able to narrow down on the correct response here.

Fill-in 2 will rely entirely on the context of the sentence and blank (i). Considering blank (i) we realize that earlier works could either have 'influenced' or been 'antithetical with'

the works of Harold. Considering each case: if earlier works were antithetical to Harold's works, then it would be incorrect to view his works as entirely **corroborative** or **supplementary** creations. On the other hand, if earlier works inspired Harold's works, it would be incorrect to view his works as entirely **original** creations. Let us check the answers to find one that matches with either of the words for **fill-in 2**.

Let us understand the meanings of the option words from blank (ii).

(D) calumnious – slandering

(E) independent – autonomous; self-made

(F) collaborative –produced by two or more parties

The correct answer for blank (ii) is 'independent' since this matches the context of original. The word 'collaborative', though close to supplementary or corroborative does not agree logically with the sentence since we are referring to poets from different time lines and it is logically impossible for them to have produced something by 'working together'. The word 'calumnious' does not fit the context of the sentence.

The correct answers are B & E.

56. Let us understand the meaning of the sentence from the partial information.

The sentence describes works of geographic description prior to Philip, suggesting that they were beautiful but rarely **something** and that they had a **particular** nature that most 18nd century geographic description had. The **hint-phrase** for both the blanks is '**kept researchers from identifying nuances**'. Therefore **fill-in 1** must be a word similar to **detailed**.

Let us understand the meanings of the option words from blank (i).

(A) traditional – existing in or as part of a tradition

(B) divisive – tending to cause disagreement or hostility between

(C) precise – marked by exactness and accuracy of expression or detail

The correct answer for blank (i) is 'precise' since this is closest in meaning to 'detailed'. The words 'divisive' and 'traditional' do not match the context required by the context.

Let us pre-empt **fill-in 2**. The **hint-phrase** here is the same as that of blank (ii). In context the word '**in accurate**' or '**lacking critical details**' will act as **fill-in 2**.

Let us understand the meanings of the option words from blank (ii).

(D) inexact – not accurate or correct

(E) reformist – supporting gradual reform

(F) expatiated – spoken or written in detail about

The word 'inexact' suits the context of the sentence. The words 'reformist' and 'expatiated' does not match the context of the sentence.

The correct answers are C & D.

57. Let us understand the meanings of the sentences from the partial information.

The sentences express the paradoxical nature of the actor's life and depict how his lifestyle is not a perfect match to the characters he plays on screen. So the sentence essentially is: The **some kinds of** characters portrayed by him on screen are a stark contrast to his utterly **some kind of** lifestyle.

Thus, we can infer that both the blanks are necessarily the opposite. These kinds of questions are either too easy or too hard; easy on a count that if you get a hint for one blank, the other follows, however if you don't, the other follows the same fate.

So, **fill-in 1** is **Some 'X'** and **fill-in 2** is **Opposite of Some 'X'**.

The **hint-phrase** is **paradox of sorts** and **signal words** – '**stark contrast to**' further help to understand the **fill-ins**.

Let us pre-empt **fill-ins**.

So, if **fill-in 1** comes from the synonym family of **bright, colorful,** etc., **fill-in 2** will take something from the family of **dull, boring, lifeless,** etc.

OR

If **fill-in 1** comes from the synonym family of **sober, serious, dry,** etc., **fill-in 2** will take something from the family of **flamboyant, extravagant**, etc.

Let us understand the meanings of the option words from blank (i).

(A) obscure – not clear; ambiguous

(B) flamboyant – ostentatious; colorful; stylish

(C) affluent – rich; wealthy

The correct answer would be 'flamboyant'. It brings in the context of bright and colorful. The other words 'obscure' and 'affluent' don't find contrasting words among the options for blank (i).

Since **fill-in 1** is 'flamboyant', **fill-in 2** must be something from the family of dull, boring, and lifeless.

Let us understand the meanings of the option words from the blank (ii).

(D) colorful – flamboyant; vibrant

(E) mawkish – excessively sentimental; overemotional

(F) vapid – dull; boring

The correct answer would be 'vapid'. While 'colorful' gives a similar meaning to blank (i), 'mawkish' can be a trap option; however, opposite to 'flamboyant' need not be sentimental.

The correct answers are B & F.

58. Let us understand the meaning of the sentence from the partial information.

The sentence discusses the Concorde and its implication on the airline industry. Blank (i) has the **hint-phrase** '**first commercial airplane to reach supersonic speeds** '. The word '**achievement**' can act as **fill-in 1**.

Fill-in 1 should be a word that relates to **achievement**.

Let us understand the meanings of the option words from blank (i).

(A) milestone – significant stage or event in the development of something

(B) regression – return to a former or less developed state

(C) cornerstone – important quality or feature on which a particular thing depends or is based; foundation

The correct answer for blank (i) is 'milestone' since this matches the context of 'achievement'. The word 'cornerstone' is very similar in meaning but on close inspection, we realize that this means the foundation or the building blocks of something; the context does not suggest that Concorde was the first airplane ever built or that it was an airplane that inspired all future airplanes. The word 'regression' is in contrast with what the sentence requires.

Let us pre-empt **fill-in 2**. The **hint-phrase 'immense influence'** and the **signal word 'although'** suggest that the initial acceptance was **underwhelming** or **bad**.

Fill-in 2 should be a word that relates to **underwhelming** or **bad**.

Let us understand the meanings of the option words from blank (ii).

(D) prodigious – great in extent; remarkable

(E) disappointing – failing to fulfill hopes or expectations

(F) trifling – unimportant or trivial

The correct answer for blank (ii) is 'disappointing'. The word 'prodigious' is opposite of what the context requires. The word 'trifling' would suggest that the commuter acceptance was unimportant – this does not agree with the context of the sentence.

The correct answers are A & E.

59. Let us understand the meanings of the sentences from the partial information.

The sentence describes Gladsone; it states that he is an expert in turning **particular** kind of things into **some kind** of events. The blanks are dependent on each other and the **hint-phrase** is found in the second sentence. The second sentence says '**seemingly mundane information can tell a beautiful story**'. Therefore we realize that he turns **boring** things into **interesting** events.

Fill-in 1 should be a word that relates to **boring**.

Let us understand the meanings of the option words from blank (i).

(A) inauspicious – gloomy; ill-fated

(B) quotidian – ordinary or every day; mundane

(C) propitious – giving or indicating a good chance of success; favorable

The correct answer for blank (i) is 'quotidian' since this brings in the context of everyday and boring. The word 'inauspicious' might seem relevant but this means to be unfavorable, the sentence does not support this in context. The word 'propitious' is also not relevant in context.

Let us pre-empt **fill-in 2**. From context we realize that the quotidian things will be changed into **interesting** things.

Let us understand the meanings of the option words from blank (ii).

(D)   picayune – of little or no value; petty

(E)   banal – lacking originality; boring

(F)   mesmerizing – capturing the complete attention of someone; transfixing

The correct answer for blank (ii) is 'mesmerizing'. The word 'banal' and 'picayune' are opposites of what the context requires.

The correct answers are B & F.

60.   Let us understand the meaning of the sentence from the partial information.

The sentence states that she felt a **certain** way about swimming, but this did not diminish her **something** to join her friends on a scuba diving trip. From context we realize that the blanks are related to each other. They share an opposing relationship. We therefore realize that **fill-in 1** could be **bad** at swimming or contrarily it could be **very good** at swimming. If she were **very bad** at swimming then **fill-in 2** would be **excitement**. Although, if **fill-in 1** were '**very good**' at swimming, there is no logical consequence that is necessarily true. i.e. "That she was very good at swimming did not reduce her lack of enthusiasm to join her friends".

Therefore, let us pre-empt **fill-in 1**. From context we realize that she was **very bad** at swimming.

Let us understand the meanings of the option words from blank (i).

(A)   attracted to – enticed into; charmed into

(B)   fearful of – afraid or; scared of

(C)   knowledgeable about – informed or learned about

The correct answer for blank (i) is 'fearful of', since this is the closest in contextual meaning to being 'bad' at swimming. The words 'attracted to' and 'knowledgeable about' create sentences that are contrary to what the context requires.

Let us pre-empt **fill-in 2**. We need a word which suggests that although she was afraid of swimming, this didn't reduce her **excitement** to join her friends.

Fill-in 2 should be a word that relates to **excitement**.

Let us understand the meanings of the option words from blank (ii).

(D)   determination – resolve; firmness of purpose

(E)   reluctance – unwillingness; dis-inclination

(F)   reservedness – slowness in revealing emotion or opinion

The correct answer for blank (ii) is 'determination', since this is closest in meaning contextually to 'excitement'. The word 'reluctance' is in contrast to what the sentence requires. The word 'reservedness' is not relevant in context.

The correct answers are B & D.

61.   Let us understand the meanings of the sentences from the partial information.

The sentence describes Martha's efforts and how the public reacted to them. The sentence says that Martha has quite <u>some way</u> become the object of both great contempt and great <u>something</u>. The context here suggests that either she became the object of two contrasting emotions or of emotions that go along with each other. Let us preempt words for each scenario and then consider those with the answer options for blank (ii). The word '<u>hate</u>' or '<u>admiration</u>' could act as <u>fill-in 2</u>.

Let us understand the meanings of the option words from blank (ii).

(D)   veneration – great reverence or respect

(E)   befuddlement – inability to think clearly

(F)   placation – lessening of anger or hostility

The correct answer for blank (ii) is 'veneration' since this goes with 'admiration'. The words 'befuddlement' and 'placation', although they sound good in context, do not agree with any of the **hints** provided in the context of the sentence.

Let us pre-empt **fill-in 1**. The sentence suggests Martha became the object of both great hatred and love. This seems quite contradictory. Although not the best **fill-in** the word, '**contradictorily**' could work as a general guideline of what could act as the right option.

Fill-in 1 should be an adjective that relates to **contradictorily**.

Let us understand the meanings of the option words from blank (i).

(A)   paradoxically – absurdly and self-contradictorily

(B)   predictably – in a way that is expected

(C)   ostensibly – supposedly true but not necessarily so

The correct answer for blank (i) is 'paradoxically' since this matches the context of 'contradictorily'. The word 'predictably' is opposite of what the context requires. The word 'ostensibly' does not match the context of the sentence.

The correct answers are A & D.

62.   Let us understand the meanings of the sentences from the partial information.

The sentence describes the theology of a particular church and suggests that while it is tolerant of other denominations (churches with similar theologies), it is a **particular way** to what it regards as **something**. The simplest blank to work with is blank (i) since there is a hint-word '**tolerant**' and signal-word '**while**' suggesting that it is **intolerant** to some other sects.

Fill-in 1 should be an adjective that relates to **intolerant**.

Let us understand the meanings of the option words from blank (i).

(A)   unapologetically indifferent – to be unconcernedly apathetic

(B)   unstintingly forgiving – to be generously forgiving

(C)   uncompromisingly hostile – to be extremely aggressive and unfriendly

The correct answer for blank (i) is 'uncompromisingly hostile' since this goes with 'intolerant'. The phrase 'unstintingly forgiving' is opposite of what the context requires. The phrase 'unapologetically indifferent' shows a lack of concern or care. This does not fit the context of the sentence since being 'intolerant' requires the lack of apathy.

Let us pre-empt **fill-in 2**. From the context of the sentence, we realize that the Church's intolerance must be targeted at sects that do not agree with their theology. Since we know that they tolerate other denominations institutions that share similar beliefs. The word '**different**' could work as **fill-in 2**.

Fill-in 2 should be an adjective that relates to **different**.

Let us understand the meanings of the option words from blank (ii).

(D) refulgent – shining very brightly

(E) heterodox – not conforming with accepted or orthodox standards or beliefs: heterodox views

(F) supercilious – behaving or looking as though one thinks one is superior to others

The correct answer for blank (ii) is 'heterodox' since this matches the context of 'different'. The word 'supercilious' though it sounds good in context does not bring in the context of 'being different' or 'having a different view-point or belief'. The word 'refulgent' is not relevant to the context of the sentence.

The correct answers are C & E.

63. Let us understand the meanings of the sentences from the partial information.

The sentence describes Georgia; it states that she was a **particular** way by nature and she found Jake's quality **something**. The **hint-phrase** for blank (i) is '**preferred to speak only when absolutely necessary**'. The word '**taciturn**' or '**not prone to talking much**' can work as **fill-in 1**.

Fill-in 1 should be an adjective that relates to **taciturn**.

Let us understand the meanings of the option words from blank (i).

(A) ebullient– cheerful and full of energy

(B) laconic – using very few word

(C) asocial – avoiding social interactions

The correct answer for blank (i) is 'laconic' since this goes with 'taciturn'. The word 'asocial' thought seems usable in context is not really relevant since the only **hint** we have is that she speaks less; asocial doesn't bring out this meaning necessarily. The word 'ebullient' is not relevant to the context of the sentence.

Let us pre-empt **fill-in 2**. From context we know that she preferred to speak less. Therefore her reaction to Jake's incessant chatter might be that of annoyance or dislike. The word '**annoying**' can therefore act as **fill-in 2**.

Fill-in 2 should be an adjective that relates to **annoying**.

Let us understand the meanings of the option words from blank (ii).

(D) discomfiting – causing uneasiness or embarrassment

(E) enchanting – delightfully charming or attractive

(F) stimulating – encouraging or arousing interest or enthusiasm

The correct answer for blank (ii) is 'discomfiting' as this does bring in a negative undertone and is related to the 'annoying'. The words 'enchanting' and 'stimulating' are both positive and are therefore opposites of what the context requires.

The correct answers are B & D.

64. Let us understand the meanings of the sentences from the partial information.

    The sentence describes how most Asians consider the words of their mentors. It states that mentors' words are considered **something** and to doubt them is considered almost **something**. There are no clear **hints** for us to come out with a **fill-in**. Let's look at the options and take a call.

    Let us understand the meanings of the option words from blank (i).

    (A) incontrovertible – cannot be denied or disputed

    (B) inevitable – certain to happen; unavoidable

    (C) excruciating – intensely painful

    For blank (i), the word 'inevitable' does not truly make logical sense: words of someone cannot be considered 'inevitable'. The words 'incontrovertible' and 'excruciating' could be possible responses.

    Let us pre-empt **fill-in 2**. From context we know that a mentor's word can either be 'excruciating' or 'incontrovertible'. For the word 'excruciating' there is no necessary conclusion we could make in context of what doubting a mentor's words would be considered. i.e. words of a mentor considered painful, and doubting it is considered (no necessary word can be produced here). On the other hand, if a mentor's word is considered 'incontrovertible' we realize that doubting his words would be considered **a bad thing**. The word '**disrespectful**' could work as **fill-in 2**.

    Fill-in 2 should be an adjective that relates to **disrespectful**.

    Let us understand the meanings of the option words from blank (ii).

    (D) sacrilegious – that which violates or misuses what is regarded sacred

    (E) reverential – characterized by deep respect for someone or something

    (F) felicitous – well-chosen or suited to the circumstances

    The correct answer for blank (ii) is 'sacrilegious' since this brings the context of 'disrespect'. The words 'reverential' and 'felicitous' are in contrast with what the sentence requires.

    From analyzing the option we realize that the correct answer for blank (i) is 'incontrovertible'.

    The correct answers are A & D.

65. Let us understand the meanings of the sentences from the partial information.

    The sentence describes the audience's reaction to the movie 'Growing Up'. For blank (ii) the **hint-phrase** is '**the only thing we know about the movie is that it portrays the experiences and emotions of teenage life very realistically**'. Though this doesn't give a very precise picture of what **fill-in 2** must be, we do understand that it needs to be a positive word.

Let us understand the meanings of the option words from blank (ii).

(D)   banally – in a way that is lacking in originality

(E)   evocatively – in a way that brings stung memories and emotions to mind

(F)   sterilely – in a way that is lacking in creativity and imagination

The correct answer for blank (ii) is 'evocatively' since this is the only positive word among the options. The words 'banally' and 'sterilely' both have a negative undertone.

Let us pre-empt **fill-in 1**. From context we realize that the audience was filled with a **particular** kind of feeling. We need a word that suggests that the adults felt strong emotion about a movie that was about childhood. Again, we would need a word that is positive in context and brings in the meaning of 'fond remembrance'.

Fill-in 1 should be an adjective that relates to '**fond remembrance**'.

Let us understand the meanings of the option words from blank (i).

(A)   animosity – strong hostility

(B)   nostalgia – a sentimental longing or wistful affection for a period in the past

(C)   ennui – a feeling of listlessness and dissatisfaction arising from a lack of occupation or excitement

The correct answer for blank (i) is 'nostalgia' as this does bring in a positive undertone in context and means 'fond remembrance'. The words 'animosity' and 'ennui' are both negative words and therefore do not fit the context of the sentence.

The correct answers are B & E.

66.   Let us understand the meanings of the sentences from the partial information.

The sentence describes Charles and his character. Blank (i) and (ii) are related to each other. The sentence says that he is well known for his **something**, and that he did not **do something** when met with open disagreement from subordinated. Since there are no clear **hint-words** let's work form the options.

Let us understand the meanings of the option words from blank (ii).

(D)   brooked – tolerated or allowed

(E)   dispatched – dealt with quickly or efficiently

(F)   condescended – showed that one feels superior

All the options can make sense in context as per the information provided in the sentence. Let us understand what words could be produced in blank (i) considering each option in blank (ii). For the word 'brooked', if he tolerated no open disagreement, Charles would be known for his **bossiness** and **arrogance**. For the word 'dispatched', if he dispatched no open disagreement, Charles would be known for his **incompetence**. For the word 'condescended', if Charles condescended no open disagreement, he would be known for his **open-mindedness** or **humility**.

Let us understand the meanings of the option words from blank (i).

(A) impetuousness – to act and do things quickly and without thought or care

(B) imperiousness – arrogant and domineering attitude

(C) equipoise – balance of forces or interests

The correct answer for blank (i) is 'imperiousness' since this matches the word 'arrogance' or 'bossiness'. The word 'impetuousness' does not match with any of the possible alternatives. The word 'equipoise' looks like it might go with 'condescended' but it does not really mean 'open-mindedness' or 'humility'.

For blank (ii) the word 'brooked' is the correct answer since it is the only one that creates a meaningful pair blank (i).

The correct answers are B & D.

67. Let us understand the meanings of the sentences from the partial information.

The sentence describes the Jackson family. They were known for not giving into **something**. None of the family members feared **something**. Blank (ii) has a more obvious **hint-phrase**: '**acting and being different from their neighbors**'.

The word '**being different**' can work as **fill-in 2**.

Let us understand the meanings of the option words from blank (ii).

(D) adulation– excessive admiration or praise

(E) insubordination – defiance of authority; refusal to obey orders

(F) singularity – distinctiveness; difference

The correct answer for blank (ii) is 'singularity' as this goes with 'being different'. The words 'adulation' and 'insubordination' do not fit the context of the sentence.

Let us pre-empt **fill-in 1**. The **hint-word 'singularity'** and the signal phrase '**not giving into**' suggests that we require a word which is opposite in meaning to 'being different or unique'. The word 'normality' could work as **fill-in 1**.

Fill-in 1 should be an adjective that relates to '**normality**'.

Let us understand the meanings of the option words from blank (i).

(A) sensibility – a quality of delicate sensitivity that makes one liable to be offended or shocked

(B) humility – the quality of having a modest or low view of one's importance

(C) conformity – compliance with standards, rules, or laws

The correct answer for blank (i) is 'conformity' since this is the closest in meaning to 'normality'. Although 'humility' sounds possible it doesn't really mean to 'be normal' or to 'not stand out' again, the opposite of 'humility' would be pride and this does not correspond with 'singularity'. The word 'sensibility' does not fit the context of the sentence.

The correct answers are C & F.

68. Let us understand the meanings of the sentences from the partial information.

The sentence states that fundamentalism destroys scientific progress and that this is supported by historic proof that scientific progress has done **something** only when fundamental religious beliefs have been **something**. For blank (i) the **hint-phrase** is the entire of the first part of the sentence "**That fundamentalism in religion destroys scientific progress**". But, this isn't by itself enough, as **fill-in 1** will depend on what **fill-in 2** is. Either way the words that can fit the context for blank (i) are either '**increased**' or '**reduced**'

Let us understand the meanings of the option words from blank (i).

(A) pandered – gratified or indulged

(B) flourished – developed rapidly and successfully

(C) fulminated – expressed vehement protest

The correct answer for blank (i) is 'flourished' as this goes with 'increased'. The words 'pandered' and 'fulminated' do not fit the context of the sentence.

Let us pre-empt **fill-in 2**. The **hint-word '**flourished**'** along with the signal phrase of blank (i) suggest that science has flourished only when fundamentalist religious beliefs have been **ignored**.

Fill-in 1 should be an adjective that relates to **ignored**.

Let us understand the meanings of the option words from blank (ii).

(D) neglected – disregarded; not paid proper attention to

(E) promoted – supported or actively encouraged

(F) patronized – given financial or other support to

The correct answer for blank (ii) is 'neglected'. The words 'promoted' and 'patronized' are opposites of what the context requires.

The correct answers are B & D.

69. Let us understand the meanings of the sentences from the partial information.

The sentence states that behaviorists have fairly clear **something** for animal behavior but not for humans. Form context we realize that blank (i) is discussing about **rules** or **guidelines**. Let's use these as **fill-in 1**.

Fill-in 1 should be an adjective that relates to **guidelines**.

Let us understand the meanings of the option words from blank (i).

(A) norms – a standard or pattern, especially of social behavior, that is typical or expected

(B) obfuscations – actions done to make something unclear or to mislead

(C) conundrums – confusing and difficult problems or questions

The correct answer for blank (i) is 'norms' as this is in line with 'rules' and 'guidelines'. The words 'obfuscations' and 'conundrums' do not fit the context of the sentence.

Let us pre-empt **fill-in 2**. The **hint-word 'clear norms'** along with the **signal phrase 'although'** suggests that there seems to be a '**lack of clarity**' about what constitutes appropriate behavior in humans.

Fill-in 2 should be a adjective that relates to **lack of clarity**.

Let us understand the meanings of the option words from blank (ii).

(D) certainty – the quality of being reliably true

(E) confusion – uncertainty about what is intended

(F) rigidity – the lack of ability to change or adapt

The correct answer for blank (ii) is 'confusion' as this matches 'lack of clarity'. The word 'certainty' is in contrast with what is required by the sentence. The word 'rigidity' is not relevant to the context of the sentence.

The correct answers are A & E.

70. Let us understand the meanings of the sentences from the partial information.

   The first sentence describes a problem that Atari Gaming Corporation faces. The gist of the problems is that the proposed release of the next version of the console has gotten people excited about it, therefore they refuse to purchase the current version. Keeping this in mind **fill-in 1** must be a word which means '**version**'.

   Fill-in 1 should be a word that relates to **version**.

   Let us understand the meanings of the option words from blank (i).

   (A) iteration – a new version of a piece of computer hardware or software

   (B) stereotype – a thing that conforms to a widely held but oversimplified image of the class or type to which it belong

   (C) legacy – something left or handed down by a predecessor

   The correct answer for blank (i) is 'iteration' since this goes with 'version'. The word 'stereotype' does not match the context of the sentence. The word 'legacy' is in contrast to what the sentence requires.

   Let us pre-empt **fill-in 2**. From context we realize that the customers aren't willing to buy the current version of the console. '**Current**' can act as **fill-in 2**.

   Fill-in 2 should be a word that relates to **current**.

   Let us understand the meanings of the option words from blank (ii).

   (D) outmoded – out dated; old fashioned

   (E) prevailing – existing at a particular time; current

   (F) parochial – having a limited or narrow outlook or scope

   The correct answer for blank (ii) is 'prevailing'. The word 'parochial' doesn't really fit the context of 'current version'. The word 'outmoded', thought it seems relevant actually isn't since the new version isn't released yet and therefore the current version cannot be 'outmoded'.

   The correct answers are A & E.

71. Let us understand the meaning of the sentence from the partial information.

   The sentence describes a shift in perception about Nikola Tesla through time. It says that he is **considered in a particular way** as one of the most prestigious minds. But, in his time **he was looked upon differently**. We realize that the **signal word 'unfortunately'** suggests a contrast in meaning between the contexts of both the blanks. From context we realize that **fill-in 1** must be '**praised**'.

Fill-in 1 should be a word that relates to **praised**.

Let us understand the meanings of the option words from blank (i).

(1) ostracized – excluded from a society or group; banished

(2) vilified – spoken or written about in an abusively disparaging manner

(3) venerated – regarded with great respect

The correct answer for blank (i) is 'venerated' since this goes with 'praised'. The words 'ostracized' and 'vilified' are opposites of what the context requires.

Let us pre-empt **fill-in 2**. From context we notice the **hint-phrase 'as a man who was not sufficiently educated to make the scientific breakthroughs that he did'**; the word '**shunned**' or '**ignored**' could make sense in context.

Fill-in 2 should be a word that relates to **shunned**.

Let us understand the meanings of the option words from blank (ii).

(D) deified – worshipped or regarded as god

(E) glorified – represented as or appearing more elevated or special than is the case

(F) dismissed – treated as unworthy of serious consideration

The correct answer for blank (ii) is 'dismissed'. The words 'deified' and 'glorified' are opposites of what the context requires.

The correct answers are C & F.

72. Let us understand the meaning of the sentence from the partial information.

The sentence describes President Obama, his actions and the public's reactions to them. The **hint-word** for blank (i) is found in '**facing**', which carries a slightly negative undertone. For instance people 'face criticism' or 'face punitive actions' no one 'faces' something rewarding or nice. Therefore we need a word, which means '**criticism**'.

Fill-in 1 should be a word that relates to **criticism**.

Let us understand the meanings of the option words from blank (i).

(A) impeachment – charging (the holder of a public office) with misconduct

(B) lionization – giving a lot of public attention and approval to (someone); treating as a celebrity

(C) denouncement – publicly declaring to be wrong or evil

The correct answer for blank (i) is 'denouncement' since this goes with 'criticism'. The word 'impeachment' goes a little beyond context since the sentence does not support the context of 'being charged with an accusation of something'. The word 'lionization' is opposite of what the sentence requires.

Let us pre-empt **fill-in 2**. From context we know that Obama was formerly criticized for his involvement in Syria. We also know that he now is facing criticism for his **something** of it (involvement in Syria). The signal phrase '**while**' suggests that while he was criticized for involving in Syria before, he is now being criticized for doing the opposite of that now. The word '**non-involvement in**' could work as **fill-in 2**.

Fill-in 2 should be a word that relates to **non-involvement in**.

Let us understand the meanings of the option words from blank (ii).

(D) solicitous interest in – showing excessive interest of concern about something

(E) lack of involvement in – not be interested or associated with something

(F) malevolent attachment to – an evil or harmful obsession or attachment to something

The correct answer for blank (ii) is 'lack of interest in'. The phrases 'solicitous interest in' and 'malevolent attachment to' both bring in a context of 'showing excessive interest' and this is opposite to what the sentence requires.

The correct answers are C & E.

73. Let us understand the meanings of the sentences from the partial information.

The sentence describes Joshua, who survived the holocausts and has a **particular** world-view. The **hint-phrase** for blank (i) is that he '**sees through the something of good manners into the animal inside of even the common-man**'. This suggests that he has a very pessimistic view of humanity. '**Pessimistic**' can therefore word as **fill-in 1**.

Fill-in 1 should be a word that relates to **pessimistic**.

Let us understand the meanings of the option words from blank (i).

(A) cynical – believing that people are motivated purely by self-interest; distrustful of human sincerity or integrity

(B) utopian – modeled on or aiming for a state in which everything is perfect; idealistic

(C) quixotic – extremely idealistic; unrealistic and impractical

The correct answer for blank (i) is 'cynical' since this goes with 'pessimism'. The words 'utopian' and 'quixotic' are opposites of what the context requires.

Let us pre-empt **fill-in 2**. From context we know that he looks past the something of good manners '**into the animal inside**'. Thus it suggests that the good manners are merely an outward appearance. The word '**outward appearance**' can act as **fill-in 2**.

Fill-in 2 should be a word that relates to **outward appearance**.

Let us understand the meanings of the option words from blank (ii).

(D) veneer – cover or disguise (someone or something's true nature) with an attractive appearance

(E) pith – the essence of something

(F) panacea – a solution or remedy for all difficulties or diseases

The correct answer for blank (ii) is 'veneer' since this goes with 'outward appearance'. The words 'pith' is opposite of what the context requires. The word 'panacea' is not relevant to the context of the sentence.

The correct answers are A & D.

74. Let us understand the meaning of the sentence from the partial information.

The sentence describes Jerome; it states that he earnestly did **something** after he had been found guilty of treason. The **hint-word** for blank (i) is the word '**earnestly**'. Therefore, '**pleaded for forgiveness**' could work as **fill-in 1**.

Fill-in 1 should be a word that relates to **pleaded for forgiveness**.

Let us understand the meanings of the option words from blank (i).

(A) hollered for retribution – shout out for punishment for someone as vengeance for a criminal or wrong act

(B) supplicated for forgiveness – beg for forgiveness

(C) genuflected with acquiescence – submit to someone or something with great cooperation and willingness

The correct answer for blank (i) is 'supplicated for forgiveness' since this goes with 'pleaded for forgiveness'. The other options are opposites of what the context requires.

Let us pre-empt **fill-in 2**. The latter part of the sentence says 'he explained the circumstances under which the act had been performed, which seemed, at least so far as he was concerned, to do **something** to the deed'. The suggested tone is that of him justifying his actions or giving an excuse for what he didn't wasn't so bad. The **hint-phrase** '**explained the circumstances under which the act had been performed**' serves as evidence for this. The word '**lessen the intensity of**' will act as **fill-in 2**.

Fill-in 2 should be a word that relates to **lessen the intensity of**.

Let us understand the meanings of the option words from blank (ii).

(D) exacerbate – make (a problem, bad situation, or negative feeling) worse

(E) extenuate – acting in mitigation to lessen the seriousness of guilt or an offense

(F) formulate – create or prepare methodically

The correct answer for blank (ii) is 'extenuate' since this goes with 'lessen the intensity of'. The word 'exacerbate' is contrary to what the sentence requires. The word 'formulate' does not fit the required context of the sentence.

The correct answers are B & E.

75. Let us understand the meanings of the sentences from the partial information.

The sentence discusses the relationship Wagner and Nietzsche shared. It states that Wagner became a **particular** presence in Nietzsche's life. The **hint-phrase** '**providing him with a model of philosophical sensibility that inspired him throughout his life**' suggests that he was a life-long influence. The word '**life-long**' can act as **fill-in 1**.

Fill-in 1 should be a word that relates to **life-long**.

Let us understand the meanings of the option words from blank (i).

(A) an enduring – long-lasting; continuing

(B) a perfidious – deceitful and untrustworthy

(C) a balking – resistant and unwilling

The correct answer for blank (i) is 'an enduring' since this matches the context of 'life-long'. The words 'a perfidious' and 'a balking' are opposites of what the context suggests about Wagner's influence.

Let us pre-empt **fill-in 2**. The context 'Nietzsche was painfully responsive to the mutability of beauty and the **something** of youth, and therefore yearned for immortality through philosophy' contains the hint-words '**mutability**' and '**yearned for immortality**'. These suggest that they were responsive to the '**temporality**' of youth.

Fill-in 2 should be a word that relates to **temporality**.

Let us understand the meanings of the option words from blank (ii).

(D)   evanescence – the quality of passing out of sight, memory, or existence; quickly fading or disappearing

(E)   caprice – the quality of changing unaccountably in mood or behavior

(F)   rapture – a feeling of intense pleasure or joy

The correct answer for blank (ii) is 'evanescence'. The words 'caprice' and 'rapture' do not fit the context that the sentence requires.

The correct answers are A & D.

76.   Let us understand the meanings of the sentences from the partial information.

The sentence describes a scenario, in which a huge company fails to pay salaries to its employees. It states that legal actions for such employees are **something**. The sentence suggests that these courses of action are present. The word '**available**' could work as **fill-in 1**.

Fill-in 1 should be a word that relates to **available**.

Let us understand the meanings of the option words from blank (i).

(A)   accessible – able to be easily obtained or used

(B)   unavailable – not able to be used or obtained

(C)   required – officially compulsory, or otherwise considered essential; indispensable

The correct answer for blank (i) is 'accessible'. The word 'unavailable' is opposite of what the sentence requires. The word 'required' does not go well with the required context of 'available'; since we already know that these legal courses of actions are present and active.

Let us pre-empt **fill-in 2**. From context we realize that although available, these legal actions are quite costly and time consuming and therefore this makes it **something** to develop other options. The word '**necessary**' could work in context.

Fill-in 2 should be a word that relates to **necessary**.

Let us understand the meanings of the option words from blank (ii).

(D)   imperative – essential or urgent

(E)   impractical – not adapted for use or action; not sensible or realistic

(F)   ridiculous – deserving or inviting derision or mockery; absurd

The correct answer for blank (ii) is 'imperative'. The words 'impractical' and 'ridiculous' are contrary to the suggested meaning of the sentence.

The correct answers are A & D.

77. Let us understand the meanings of the sentences from the partial information.

The sentence describes the perception that modern astronomers have about the views of pre-Galilean astronomers. The **hint-word 'irrelevant'** serves to suggest that they have a negative opinion about the same. Let us look at the options for blank (i) and isolate those that have a negative undertone.

Let us understand the meanings of the option words from blank (i).

(A) obsolete – no longer produced or used; out of date

(B) theoretical – concerned with or involving the theory of a subject or area of study rather than its practical application

(C) sapient – wise, or attempting to appear wise

The correct answer for blank (i) is 'obsolete' and fits well in the context of 'old and out dated views of scientists'. The word 'theoretical' is neutral and the word 'sapient' is positive in context, therefore these words do not match the required context of the sentence.

Let us pre-empt **fill-in 2**. From context we realize that modern astronomers perceive these old views as only a **particular** kind of interest. Since we know that the views are considered **'obsolete'** and **'irrelevant'** they must be considered something of **'non-important'** interest.

Fill-in 2 should be a word that relates in context to the word **non-important**.

Let us understand the meanings of the option words from blank (ii).

(D) historical – of or concerning history or past events

(E) seminal – strongly influencing later developments

(F) sartorial – relating to tailoring, clothes, or style of dress

The correct answer for blank (ii) is 'historical'; although this does not mean non-important, in context it does convey a meaning of something that isn't fundamentally important to that of what astronomy is; the history of most fields is of peripheral interest after all when compared to the core science within them. The word 'seminal' is opposite of what the context requires. The word 'sartorial' is not relevant to the context of the sentence.

The correct answers are A & D.

78. Let us understand the meanings of the sentences from the partial information.

The sentence describes Ferguson's involvement in the new legislative reform. The sentence provides the **hint-phrase 'bringing into actualization...'** suggesting that he was a **supporter** of the legal reform.

Fill-in 1 should be a word that relates to **supporter**.

Let us understand the meanings of the option words from blank (i).

(A) debaser – someone who works toward reducing the quality or value of something

(B) proponent – a person who advocates a theory, proposal, or course of action

(C) heckler – someone who interrupts (a public speaker) with derisive or aggressive comments or abuse

The correct answer for blank (i) is 'proponent'. The word 'debaser' is opposite of what the sentence requires. The word 'heckler' does not fit the required context of the sentence.

Let us pre-empt **fill-in 2**. We realize that Ferguson was not only the supporter, but also was **something** that various aspects of the reform into actualization. The word '**promoter**' or '**helper**' can work here.

Fill-in 2 should be a word that relates to **helper**.

Let us understand the meanings of the option words from blank (ii).

(D) catalyst – a person or thing that precipitates an event

(E) filibuster – a person engaging in unauthorized warfare against a foreign state

(F) matron – a woman in charge of domestic and medical arrangements at a boarding school or other institution

The correct answer for blank (ii) is 'catalyst' as this is relevant in context to 'helper'. The word 'filibuster' is sort of opposite of what the sentence requires. The word 'matron' does not match the context of the sentence.

The correct answers are B & D.

79. Let us understand the meanings of the sentences from the partial information.

The sentence states that all its reviewers felt amazement and marvel looking at the artistic collection of Harold. Harold received a **particular** kind of **something** from critics. The **hint-words** '**amazement**' and '**marvel**' suggest very positive reactions. Looking at the options we realize that we are to pick a set of words that complement each other to bring out the meaning of amazement and marvel.

Let us understand the meanings of the option words from blank (i).

(A) reserved – slow to reveal emotion or opinions

(B) unstinting – given or giving without restraint; unsparing

(C) belligerent – hostile and aggressive

Let us understand the meanings of the option words from blank (ii).

(D) approbation – approval or praise

(E) hostility – hostile behavior; unfriendliness or opposition

(F) criticism – the expression of disapproval of someone or something on the basis of perceived faults or mistakes

The correct answer for blank (ii) is 'approbation'. The words 'hostility' and 'criticism' are opposites of what the sentence requires.

For blank (i) the word 'unstinting' goes well with 'approbation' to fit the required context of 'amazement' and 'marvel'. The word 'reserved' doesn't bring in the required positive undertone observed in 'every single reviewer...' The word 'belligerent' has a negative undertone and cannot fit the context of the sentence.

The correct answers are B & D.

80. Let us understand the meanings of the sentences from the partial information.

    The sentence describes the behavior of dogs and how the behaviors of the owners can influence this. The first part of the sentence states that a calm, assertive master can do **something** to an insecure and nervous dog. The latter part of the sentence suggests that a master who is not calm or assertive can make a nervous and insecure dog become **something**. The contrast between a calm and not so calm master suggests that a calm one can soothe a dog; while a master who doesn't project confidence could make a dog worse. The word '**made less bad**' could work as **fill-in 1**.

    Fill-in 1 should be a word that relates to **made less bad**.

    Let us understand the meanings of the option words from blank (i).

    (A) aggravated – made more severe

    (B) settled – made calmer

    (C) aggrandized – increased the power, status or wealth of

    The correct answer for blank (i) is 'settled'. The word 'aggravated' is opposite of what the sentence requires. The word 'aggrandize' does not match the required context.

    Let us pre-empt **fill-in 2**. From context we realize that since calm masters make dogs feel calmer, not so confident masters make the condition of the dog worse. In the context, the dog's insecurities might become **worsened**.

    Fill-in 2 should be a word that relates to **worsened**.

    Let us understand the meanings of the option words from blank (ii).

    (D) inconsequential – not important or significant

    (E) mollified – appeased the anger or anxiety of

    (F) amplified – made more intense

    The correct answer for blank (ii) is 'amplified'. The word 'mollified' is opposite of what the context requires. The word 'inconsequential' doesn't match the context of the sentence.

    The correct answers are B & F.

3-blanks TC questions

81. Let us understand the meanings of the sentences from the partial information.

The sentences asserts that men have a single, relatively simple and effective measure for contraception; the second part of the sentence—'women are afforded a _____ of alternatives that suit their lifestyles, sexual appetites, and personal habits.'— is a convoluted part. With the presence of **signal word-while**, we can infer that women may have varied and relatively complex measures for contraception. We leave **fill-in 1** till we understand another sentence.

The sentence starts with another **signal word—However**, and a **hint-phrase 'for women's sake'**, thus we can infer that the author may be justifying women's varied and relatively complex needs for contraception. Later, it advocates that this **something** of options should never be viewed as too varied or as **something**.

Let us pre-empt the **fill-ins**. **fill-in 1** should be relatable synonymous words for 'lot'; **fill-in 2** should be relatable synonymous words for 'bundle'; and **fill-in 3** should be relatable synonymous words for 'extravagant'.

Let us understand the meanings of the option words from the blanks (i).

(A) plethora – excess; many

(B) dearth – lack; deficiency

(C) vestige – small or trace amounts

The correct answer is 'plethora'. While 'dearth' is opposite of what we need, 'vestige' is not relevant in the context.

Let us understand the meanings of the option words from the blanks (ii).

(D) habiliment – clothes as worn in a particular profession, way of life, etc.

(E) hodgepodge – heterogeneous mixture; variety

(F) dearth – a scarcity or lack of something

The correct answer is 'hodgepodge'. 'Habiliment' and 'dearth' are not relevant.

Let us understand the meanings of the option words from the blanks (iii).

(G) repugnant – obscene; offensive

(H) deleterious – harmful; damaging

(I) supernumerary – excessive; redundant

The correct answer is 'supernumerary'. 'Deleterious' and 'repugnant' are not relevant.

The correct answers are A, E & I.

82. Let us understand the meanings of the sentences from the partial information.

The sentences describe Aston: what was done to him, how he reacted, and how his reaction was perceived. The simplest blank to work with is blank (i). The **hint-word** for blank (i) is the word **'victim to'**. He was probably victim to several soundings or abuses from his superiors. The word **abuses** will act as **fill-in 1**.

Let us understand the meanings of the option words from blank (i).

(A) approbations – approval or praise

(B) castigations – severe scolding

(C) insubordinations – refusals to obey orders

The correct answer for blank (i) is 'castigations'. The word 'approbation' is opposite to what the context of the sentence requires. The word 'insubordination' is used to describe disrespect of a superior, since Aston is not the superior in this context, the word does not match what is required.

Let us pre-empt **fill-in 2**. From context we know that, although he was severely rebuked, he put up a **particular** kind of appearance. The signal word **although** suggests that he put up a **brave** appearance: this will work as **fill-in 2**.

Let us understand the meanings of the option words from blank (ii).

(D) composed – having one's feelings and expression under control

(E) distressed – sorrowful; painful

(F) apathetic – feeling no interest, enthusiasm, or concern

The correct answer for blank (ii) is 'composed' as this is closest in meaning to brave. The word 'distressed' is opposite to what the context requires. The word 'apathetic' brings in the meaning that's close to what the sentence requires but it has a negative undertone that suggests that he is indifferent to the actions of the superiors; this is not true when seen in context.

Let us pre-empt **fill-in 3**. From context we know that his colleagues mistook his courage for **something**. The **hint-words** '**unfortunately**' and '**rather than as**' suggests that they viewed it as a negative quality. There is no specific **fill-in** for this blank; therefore, let us eliminate answer options that do not bring in the negative undertone required by the sentence.

Let us understand the meanings of the option words from blank (iii).

(G) callousness – insensitivity towards others' feelings

(H) propriety – decorum; decency

(I) competence – ability to do something successfully or effectively

The correct answer for blank (iii) is 'callousness'. The words 'propriety' and 'competence' have a positive undertone, which do not match the context required by the sentence.

The correct answers are B, D & G.

83. Let us understand the meaning of the sentence from the partial information.

The sentence describes the new code of ethics: it suggests that the code of ethics is **something** and does not offer any perspective but the obvious. The context provides a negative undertone. There are no real **hint-words** for **fill-in 1**, but we do know that the word must be a negative one. Let us therefore evaluate the options and make a decision based on the same.

Let us understand the meanings of the option words from blank (i).

(A) indubitable – impossible to doubtable

(B) laughable – ridiculous; absurd

(C) compendious – pithy, short and to the point

The correct answer for blank (i) is 'laughable' since this is the only option that brings a negative undertone. The other options bring a positive meaning in context.

Let us pre-empt **fill-in 2**. From context we know that the guidelines are in a **particular** way. The hint-phrase here is **"offering no perspective but the obvious."** The words **'obvious'** or **'unoriginal'** can work as **fill-in 2**.

Fill-in 2 should be a word that relates to **obvious** or **unoriginal**.

Let us understand the meanings of the option words from blank (ii).

(D) platitudinous – used too often to be interesting or thoughtful; hackneyed

(E) homogenous – of the same kind; alike

(F) corroborative – used to give supporting evidence to

The correct answer for blank (ii) is 'platitudinous', since this matches the words 'obvious' or 'unoriginal' in context. The word 'homogenous' implies similarity in quality – this doesn't make sense in context since the code of ethics cannot be homogenous, furthermore the negative undertone needed for this blank is not carried in the word 'homogeneous'. Similarly, the word 'corroborative' does not bring the negative undertone that is required in context.

Let us pre-empt **fill-in 3**. From context we realize that the code of ethics does not offer any specific advice and therefore makes any action **something**. The **hint-phrase** here is **'so devoid of specific advice'**. When any rule or guideline lacks in specific advice, it permits room for people to get away with many things through loopholes it might have. Similarly, the code of ethics, because it is devoid of specific advice, might make almost any action – **'okay'**.

Fill-in 3 should be a word that relates to **okay**.

Let us understand the meanings of the option words from blank (iii).

(G) unacceptable – not satisfactory or allowable

(H) justifiable – able to be shown to be right or reasonable; defensible

(I) impartial – treating all rivals or disputants equally

The correct answer for blank (iii) is 'justifiable' since it matches the context of making any action 'okay'. The word 'unacceptable' is in contrast with what the sentence requires. The word 'impartial' is not relevant to the context of the sentence.

The correct answers are B, D, & H.

84. Let us understand the meanings of the sentences from the partial information.

The sentences describe the killer whales; they suggest that they are a **particular** kind of animals. The **hint** for **Fill-in 1** is the entire context of the sentences. The theme of them working together and being a social group suggests that they are **social** animals.

Fill-in 1 should be a word that relates to **social**.

Let us understand the meanings of the option words from blank (i).

(A) gregarious – fond of company; sociable

(B) effeminate – man having characteristics regarded as typical of a woman; unmanly

(C) sanctimonious – making a show of being morally superior to others

The correct answer for blank (i) is 'gregarious' since this is the only option that brings in the meaning of 'social'. The words 'sanctimonious' and 'effeminate' are not relevant in context.

Let us pre-empt **fill-in 2**. Again, the **hint** is contextual: we need a word that is supported by any of the details provided in the sentences.

Let us understand the meanings of the option words from blank (ii).

(D) ephemeral – lasting a very short time

(E) enduring – lasting over a long period of time; durable

(F) unorthodox – contrary to what is usual, traditional, or accepted

The correct answer for blank (ii) is 'enduring', since the sentence suggests that the killer whales live all their lives together and have a very long lasting social bond. The word 'ephemeral' is in contrast to what the sentence suggests. The word 'unorthodox' is not relevant to the context of the sentence.

Let us pre-empt **fill-in 3**. From context we realize that the families and societies are **female centered,** as the **hint-phrase** here is '**female whales live the longest and know the most, and their descendants live with them forever**'.

Fill-in 3 should be a word that relates to **female centered**.

Let us understand the meanings of the option words from blank (iii).

(G) matriarchal – a societal system with a female head

(H) anarchic – with no controlling rules or principles to give order

(I) unscrupulous – having or showing no moral principles; not honest or fair

The correct answer for blank (iii) is 'matriarchal'. The word 'anarchic' does not make sense in context since there is a clear social structure and order in the killer whale society. The word 'unscrupulous' is not relevant to the context of the sentence.

The correct answers are A, E, & G.

85. Let us understand the meanings of the sentence from the partial information.

The sentence describes Ronald, it states that he is a **particular** kind of liar and could make even the most far-fetched lies sound **some way**. Yet, he couldn't make his truth sound believable. Through context we realize that Ronald was very good a lying. He was therefore **a skilled** liar.

Fill-in 1 should be a word that relates to **a skilled**.

Let us understand the meanings of the option words from blank (i).

(A) a gauche – unsophisticated and socially awkward

(B) a fallacious – based on mistaken belief

(C) an adroit – clever and skillful

The correct answer for blank (i) is 'an adroit'. The words 'a gauche' and 'a fallacious' does not match the required context.

Let us pre-empt **fill-in 2**. Again, the **hint** in contextual: we realize that he was very good at lying and therefore he could make even the most far-fetched lies sound **believable**.

Fill-in 2 should be a word that relates to **believable**.

Let us understand the meanings of the option words from blank (ii).

(D) plausible – seeming reasonable or probable

(E) grandiose – extravagantly or pretentiously imposing in appearance or style

(F) insincere – not expressing genuine feelings

The correct answer for blank (ii) is 'plausible', since this is in line with the context of making lies sound believable. The word 'insincere' is in contrast to what the sentence requires. The word 'grandiose' will not make sense in context since making a lie grandiose does not make it sound more believable (in fact it would do the opposite).

Let us pre-empt **fill-in 3**. The sentence suggests that he could not make truth sound believable and this did **something** to him. The word '**irritated**' or '**angered**' could work as **fill-in 3**.

Fill-in 3 should be a word that relates to **irritated**.

Let us understand the meanings of the option words from blank (iii).

(G) frustrated – exasperated; annoyed

(H) placated – made less angry; appeased

 (I) distraught – devastated; shattered

The correct answer for blank (iii) is 'frustrated'. The word 'placated' is opposite of what the context requires. The word 'distraught' suggests being sorrowful beyond all hopes, this is very extreme and does not match the context of 'irritated'.

The correct answers are C, D, & G.

86. Let us understand the meaning of the sentence from the partial information.

The sentence describes hydrothermal vents and discusses how microbiologists look at them. Blank (i) requires us to understand the other two blanks. Therefore, let's start with either of the other blanks. From context we realize that hydrothermal vents **do something** to the enormously large assortment of microbial complexity. Since there are no clear **hint-words,** let's look at the answer options for blank (ii) and take a call.

Let us understand the meanings of the option words from blank (ii).

(D) relegated to – assign to an inferior rank

(E) reduced to – make small or less in amount

(F) aggrandized with – increase the power, status, or wealth of

The correct answer for blank (i) is 'reduced to'. This is because 'relegated to' cannot work since we are talking about 'complexity' and not some entity or being. Similarly, the word 'aggrandized with' cannot work in this context since 'complexity' cannot increase in status, wealth, or power.

Let us pre-empt **fill-in 3**. Since the enormously large assortment of species complexity is reduced to **some kind** of complexity, the result must be that it is reduced to a 'smaller' or 'manageable' complexity. The **hint-word 'enormously'** also suggests that something opposite to that happens. Therefore **'smaller'** or **'manageable'** can act as **fill-in 3**.

Fill-in 3 should be a word that relates to **smaller** or **manageable**.

Let us understand the meanings of the option words from blank (iii).

(G) tractable – easy to deal with

(H) diverse – showing a great deal of variety; very different

(I) intimidating – frightening; terrifying

The correct answer for blank (iii) is 'tractable', since this is in line with the context of manageable. The word 'diverse' and 'intimidating' are in contrast with what the sentence requires.

Let us pre-empt **fill-in 1**. Since the sentences suggest that an enormous assortment of microbe complexity is reduced to a manageable complexity, microbiologists must like or prefer these hydrothermal vents. Blank (i) acts as the biggest **hint-word** here. The word **'like'** or **prefer'** will be **fill-in 1**.

Fill-in 1 should be a word that relates to **'like'** or **prefer'**.

Let us understand the meanings of the option words from blank (i).

(A) detested – disliked intensely

(B) ignored – refused to take notice of or acknowledge

(C) prized – valued extremely highly

The correct answer for blank (i) is 'prized'. The word 'detested' and 'ignored' are opposites of what the context requires.

The correct answers are C, E, & G.

87. Let us understand the meaning of the sentence from the partial information.

The sentence discusses ancient scrolls (documents; manuscript), and that they were preserved a **particular** way; these showcase a particular quality about the progress of literary thought and philosophy. Blank (i) is the simplest to work with, the **hint-phrase** to help with **fill-in 1** is "**enough have survived**"; this is acted on by the **signal word 'though'**. The phrase '**not very well**' preserved or '**not often**' preserved can act as the **fill-in**.

Fill-in 1 should be a word that relates to **not very well** or **not often**.

Let us understand the meanings of the option words from blank (i).

(A) unwittingly – not done with purpose; unintentionally

(B) seldom – not often; rarely

(C) meticulously – carefully and precisely

The correct answer for blank (i) is 'seldom' since this matches the context of 'not often'. The word 'unwittingly' suggests that it was preserved but without intention, and therefore doesn't really match the required context. The word 'meticulously' is opposite of what the sentence requires.

Let us pre-empt **fill-in 3**. From context we know that there exists an occasionally inter-rupted but a generally **some kind** of progress in literature. The **hint-phrase "occasion-ally interrupted but generally..."** suggests that the progress was **existing** in spite of occasional interruptions.

Fill-in 3 should be a word that relates to **existing**.

Let us understand the meanings of the option words from blank (iii).

(G)   documented – recorded

(H)   incessant – ceaseless; perpetual

 (I)   noticeable – observable

The correct answer for blank (iii) is 'noticeable'. There is no evidence in the sentence that the progress was 'documented'. 'Documented' does not match the context of the sen-tence. The word 'incessant' goes against the meaning of the sentence since the sentence suggests that there were occasional interruptions.

Let us pre-empt **fill-in 2**. From the context we realize that the scrolls help us see that gradual literary progress existed. In other words they help us realize the existence of literary progress. The word "**realize**" will work as **fill-in 2**.

Fill-in 2 should be a word that relates to **realize**.

Let us understand the meanings of the option words from blank (ii).

(D)   coruscate – flash or sparkle

(E)   demonstrate – clearly show existence of

(F)   controvert – deny the truth of

The correct answer for blank (ii) is 'demonstrate', although this does not mean realize, it brings out the meaning that the scrolls bring to light the existence of literary progress. The words 'coruscate' is not relevant in context; the word 'controvert' is opposite of what the context requires.

The correct answers are B, E, & I.

88.   Let us understand the meaning of the sentence from the partial information.

The sentence discusses a kind of behavior and contrasts public opinion of the same now and in the past. Blank (i) is the easiest to work with; it has the hint-phrase **even a sign of madness**. **Fill-in 1** therefore must be a negative word, which addresses mental instability. The phrase **a sign of instability** can work here.

Fill-in 1 should be a word that relates to **a sign of instability**.

Let us understand the meanings of the option words from blank (i).

(A)   frivolous – not having any serious purpose or value

(B)   perspicacious – having a ready insight into and understanding of things

(C)   sociopathic – having a personality disorder manifesting itself in extreme antisocial attitudes and behavior

The correct answer for blank (i) is 'sociopathic', since this is the closest in meaning to 'a sign of instability'. The words 'frivolous' and 'perspicacious' do not match what is required by the context.

For blanks (i) and (ii), we realize that context for both refers to the same thing. The phrase 'someone directly does **something** to a generally accepted system of values' is actually referred to when the sentence says such **some kind** of behavior was idolized. Let's therefore look at the answer options and take a call on the options that can work.

Let us understand the meanings of the option words from blank (ii).

(D) legislates – make and enacts a law

(E) flouts – openly disregards something; go against

(F) acquiesces – accepts something without protest

Looking at the context we realize that 'flouts and 'acquiesces' are both possible answers. The word 'legislates' is not relevant to the context of the sentence.

Let us understand the meanings of the option words from blank (iii).

(G) delusional – maintaining an impression or belief that is contradicted by reality or logical argument

(H) iconoclastic – criticizing or attacking cherished beliefs or institutions

(I) conservative – averse to change or innovation and holding traditional values

Since blanks (ii) and (iii) are parallel to each other. Let's see which of the options can make a pair. We may thing that 'acquiesces' to generally accepted values could make a person 'conservative' but this is not necessary since conservative suggests that one is against change of the old ways, not that they necessary follow these values without protest. A better alternative is 'flouts' and 'iconoclastic' since flouting of values essentially makes a person iconoclastic. The word 'delusional' does not have any necessary relationship with options from blank (i).

The correct answers are C, E, & H.

89. Let us understand the meanings of the sentences from the partial information.

The sentences discuss Damon's feelings about acting in the movie "The Martian." The sentences state that he felt a **certain way**. The simpler blanks to work with are blank (ii) and (iii). In blank (ii), the **hint-phrase 'humor and suspenseful survival story'** suggests that he felt positively about involving in the movie. The word **exciting** works as **fill-in 2**

Fill-in 2 should be a word that relates to **exciting**.

Let us understand the meanings of the option words from blank (ii).

(D) stimulating – encouraging or arousing interest or enthusiasm

(E) laconic – using very few words

(F) hackneyed – having been overused; unoriginal and trite

The correct answer for blank (ii) is 'stimulating', since this is closest in meaning in context to 'exciting'. The word 'hackneyed' is opposite of what the sentence requires. The word 'laconic' is not relevant in context.

Let us pre-empt **fill-in 3**. The **signal phrases 'on the one hand'** and '**on the other hand**' suggest a contrast between the opinions felt within the sentences. Since he initially found the prospect stimulating, he must therefore find the other aspect of the prospect not so appealing. This must therefore have had him **thinking twice** about the prospect.

Fill-in 3 should be a word that relates to **thinking twice**.

Let us understand the meanings of the option words from blank (iii).

(G)   give pause – cause someone to think carefully or hesitate before doing something

(H)   dive in headfirst – engage in something without sufficient forethought

(I)   fired up – inflame with enthusiasm, anger, or another strong emotion

The correct answer for blank (iii) is 'give pause', since this is in line with the context of thinking twice. The phrases 'dive in head first' and 'fired up' bring a meaning that is in contrast with what the context requires.

Let us pre-empt **fill-in 1**. Since we realize that Damon had two conflicting feelings simultaneously about the prospect, he possibly had mixed feelings about it. The word '**indecisive**' can work as **fill-in 1**.

Fill-in 1 should be a word that relates to '**indecisive**'.

Let us understand the meanings of the option words from blank (i).

(A)   incensed – very angry; enraged

(B)   ambivalent – having mixed feelings or contradictory ideas about something or someone

(C)   determined – possessing or displaying resolve

The correct answer for blank (i) is 'ambivalent' since this shows that he felt mixed and is close to the meaning of the word 'indecisive'. The word 'incensed' is not relevant to the context of the sentence. 'Determined' is opposite of what the sentence requires.

The correct answers are B, D, & G.

90.   Let us understand the meaning of the sentence from the partial information.

The sentence describes a beehive. It states that worker bees are sterile (hygienic) females, acting as **something**, as the **some kind** of queen produces enough **something**. The **hint-phrase** for blank (i) is that they '**supply the colony with food**'. This suggests that they act as some kind of **workers**.

Fill-in 1 should be a word that relates to **workers**.

Let us understand the meanings of the option words from blank (i).

(A)   sentries – guards; sentinels

(B)   sages – very wise people

(C)   laborers – workers

The correct answer for blank (i) is 'laborers' since this matches the context of 'workers'. The word 'sentries' and 'sages' are not relevant to the context of the sentence.

Let us pre-empt **fill-in 3**. From context we know that the queen produces enough **something** to '**continually populate the colony**'; this is the **hint-phrase** for blank (iii). The word '**baby bees**' or '**eggs**' could work in context.

Fill-in 3 should be a word that relates to **baby bees** or **eggs**.

Let us understand the meanings of the option words from blank (iii).

(G) progeny – a descendant or the descendants of a person, animal, or plant; offspring

(H) ancestors – an early type of animal or plant from which others have evolved

(I) harbingers – a person or thing that announces or signals the approach of another

The correct answer for blank (iii) is 'progeny'. The word 'ancestor' is logically impossible, since ancestors cannot be 'produced'. The word 'harbingers' is not relevant to the context of the sentence.

Let us pre-empt **fill-in 2**. From the context we realize that the queen produces a lot of offspring. Also the word 'sterile' contrasts the role of the worker. Therefore, this suggests that the queen is **fertile** or **capable of reproducing**.

Fill-in 2 should be a word that relates to **fertile**.

Let us understand the meanings of the option words from blank (ii).

(D) fecund – highly fertile

(E) captious – tending to find fault or raise petty objections

(F) abominable – causing moral revulsion

The correct answer for blank (ii) is 'fecund' since this is in line with the context of 'fertile'. The words 'captious' and 'abominable' are not relevant to the context of the sentence.

The correct answers are C, D, & G.

91. Let us understand the meaning of the sentence from the partial information.

The sentence states that the mayor did **something** to the opposition. The **hints** in this sentence are completely contextual. From context we realize that the mayor is defending his proposal and that he shows that his plan works. With this in mind we realize that: not only has he **proved** that revamping the health plan will be successful... This will act as **fill-in 2**.

Fill-in 2 should be a word that relates to **proved**.

Let us understand the meanings of the option words from blank (ii).

(D) insinuated – suggested or hinted in an indirect and unpleasant way

(E) demonstrated – clearly showed the existence or truth of (something) by giving proof or evidence

(F) divagated – strayed or digressed

The correct answer for blank (i) is 'demonstrated' since this matches the context of 'proved'. The word 'insinuated' has a negative undertone and therefore does not match the context of the sentence. The word 'divagated' is sort of opposite of what the sentence requires.

Let us pre-empt **fill-in 3**. From context we know that 'it would achieve exactly what his proposal had **said** or **suggested** it would'. These can work as **fill-in 3**.

Fill-in 3 should be a word that relates to **suggested** or **said**.

Let us understand the meanings of the option words from blank (iii).

(G) equivocated – used ambiguous language so as to conceal the truth or avoid committing oneself

(H) prognosticated – forecasted; predicted

(I) disabused – persuaded (someone) that an idea or belief is mistaken

The correct answer for blank (iii) is 'prognosticated', since this is the closest in meaning to the word 'suggested' in context. The word 'equivocated' has a negative undertone, which is not supported by the context. The word 'disabused' is not really relevant since the context is of 'suggesting' something and not to 'correct' somebody's misconception.

Let us pre-empt **fill-in 1**. From the context we realize that the mayor **disproved** the opposition. This will act as **fill-in 1**.

Fill-in 1 should be a word that relates to **disproved**.

Let us understand the meanings of the option words from blank (i).

(A) refuted – disproved; proved wrong

(B) vindicated – cleared (someone) of blame or suspicion

(C) instigated – brought about or initiated (an action or event)

The correct answer for blank (i) is 'refuted' since this is in line with the context of 'disproved'. The word 'vindicated' is sort of contrary to what the context requires. The word 'instigated' does not match the context of the sentence.

The correct answers are A, E, & H.

92. Let us understand the meaning of the sentence from the partial information.

    The sentence describes some kind of kingdoms, the image they project and what happens to them when things go bad. Blank (ii) has the **hint-phrase 'how delicate their ecology of power is'**. This suggests that most empires are actually **delicate** or **weak** organisms.

    Fill-in 2 should be a word that relates to **delicate**.

    Let us understand the meanings of the option words from blank (ii).

    (D) macroscopic – pertaining to large units; comprehensive

    (E) insuperable – impossible to overcome

    (F) fallible – capable of making mistakes or being wrong

    The correct answer for blank (ii) is 'fallible' since this matches the context of 'weak' or 'delicate'. Though 'macroscopic' is relevant to the context, it is not in line with the pre-empted word 'delicate'. The word 'insuperable' is opposite of what the context requires.

    Let us pre-empt **fill-in 1**. From context we know that the empires project an image of **something**. But this is contrary to what they actually are: delicate and fragile. The presence of the signal word '**despite**' suggests this contrast. Therefore, these empires must be projecting an image of **power** and **might**.

__Fill-in 1__ should be a word that relates to __power__.

Let us understand the meanings of the option words from blank (i).

(A) ineptitude – having or showing no skill; clumsy

(B) omnipotence – the quality of having unlimited or very great power

(C) animosity – strong hostility

The correct answer for blank (i) is 'omnipotence', since this is the closest in meaning to the word 'power' in context. The word 'ineptitude' is opposite of what the context requires. The word 'animosity' though seems relevant actually means to be hostile and aggressive and does not mean 'power' in context.

Let us pre-empt __fill-in 3__. From the context we realize that when things go truly bad, these delicate empires do __something__ regularly. The __hint-word__ here is '__delicate__' and that delicate things would __fall apart__ or __break down__ when things go truly bad.

__Fill-in 3__ should be a word that relates to __fall apart__ or __break down__.

Let us understand the meanings of the option words from blank (iii).

(G) proliferate – increase rapidly in number

(H) pullulate – breed or spread prolifically or rapidly

(I) unravel – become undone

The correct answer for blank (i) is 'unravel' since this is in line with the context of 'break down' and 'fall apart'. The words 'pullulate' and 'proliferate' are opposites of what the context requires since they bring in the context of 'growth'.

__The correct answers are B, F, & I.__

93. Let us understand the meaning of the sentence from the partial information.

The sentence describes actions of the CEO of Cyber-con. There are no clear __hint-words__ in the sentence. Yet, the overall context can help us identify the underlying tone of the sentence. Blank (iii) suggests that the new product has gained __something__ among startups and rapidly growing IT firms. The __something__ here could be either a negative or a positive. Let us consider each possibility and work with the blanks to find out which answer options could make sense.

Therefore, the possible __fill-ins__ for blank (iii) are either __recognition__ or __criticism__.

__Fill-in 3__ should be a word that relates to either __recognition__ or __criticism__.

Let us understand the meanings of the option words from blank (iii).

(G) disrepute – the state of being held in low esteem by the public

(H) diminution – a reduction in the size, extent, or importance of something

(I) currency – the fact or quality of being generally accepted or in use

For blank (iii) the word 'diminution' does not fit the context of the sentence. 'Disrepute' goes with 'criticism' and 'currency' goes with 'recognition'. Therefore 'disrepute' and 'currency' are possible answers.

For blank (i) let us consider the possible alternatives. The CEO did __something__ to the increasingly concerned investors. This relies on blank (iii). If blank (iii) is disrepute, he made the investors more paranoid. If blank (iii) is currency, he made the investors calm. Therefore the answer must be either **'shocked'** or **'calmed'**.

Fill-in 1 should be a word that relates to **shocked** or **calmed**.

Let us understand the meanings of the option words from blank (i).

(A)   excoriated – criticized (someone) severely

(B)   vilified – spoke or wrote about in an abusively disparaging manner

(C)   placated – made (someone) less angry or hostile

The correct answer for blank (i) is 'placated' since this goes with 'calmed'. While 'excoriated' and 'vilified' are negative words, they do not mean to 'shocked' or 'made more paranoid'; and in context, the two words don't really make sense because the CEO (from context) has no reason to excoriate or vilify the investors.

This brings us back to blank (iii); since the only alternative to blank (i) was calmed, blank (iii) must be **currency**.

For **fill-in 2** we know that the CEO calmed the investors saying that despite the new product's many **something** it has gained currency in the relevant target groups. The word we need must therefore be negative because of the use of signal word **'despite'**. The word **'opponents'** makes sense in context.

Fill-in 2 should be a word that relates to **opponents**.

Let us understand the meanings of the option words from blank (ii).

(D)   proponents – people who advocate a theory, proposal, or course of action

(E)   detractors – people who disparage someone or something

(F)   exponents – people who support an idea or theory and tries to persuade people of its truth or benefits

The correct answer for blank (ii) is 'detractors'. The words 'proponent' and 'exponents' are both opposites of what the sentence requires.

The correct answers are C, E, & I.

94.   Let us understand the meaning of the sentence from the partial information.

The sentence states that being **someone** makes it difficult to make **some kind** of decisions that is required in **some kind** of corporate environment. We realize through context that all three blanks are related in theme and will carry a meaning that is parallel to each other. Let us look at the options and take a call.

Let us understand the meanings of the option words from blank (i).

(A)   intellect – a clever person

(B)   idealist – a person who is guided more by ideals than by practical considerations

(C)   elitist – a person who has superior intellect or talent, power, wealth, or membership in the upper echelons of society

Let us understand the meanings of the option words from blank (ii).

(D)   dysfunctional – operating abnormally or improperly

(E) evenhanded – fair and impartial in treatment or judgment

(F) hardheaded – practical and realistic; not sentimental

Looking at the options we see the following words that could work together: intellect and dysfunctional, idealist and hardheaded, elitist and evenhanded. But when you consider closely, it isn't necessary that an intellect will find it hard to make dysfunctional decisions or that an elitist will have a hard time making evenhanded decisions. There is no solid proof in the sentence to suggest either of this. But, an 'idealist' will have a hard time making 'hardheaded' decisions. These are therefore the correct answers for blank (i) and (ii) respectively.

For **fill-in 3** we realize that the hint-words are 'idealist' and 'hardheaded'; we need a word that is parallel in meaning to this. The word '**practicality focused**' could work as **fill-in 3.**

Fill-in 3 should be a word that relates to **practicality focused**.

Let us understand the meanings of the option words from blank (iii).

(G) pragmatic – dealing with things sensibly and realistically in a way that is based on practical rather than theoretical considerations

(H) esoteric – intended for or likely to be understood by only a small number of people with a specialized knowledge or interest

(I) parsimonious – very unwilling to spend money or use resources

The correct answer for blank (iii) is 'pragmatic'. The words 'parsimonious' and 'esoteric' are both not relevant to the context of the sentence.

The correct answers are B, F, & G.

95. Let us understand the meaning of the sentence from the partial information.

The sentence states that the court **did something** to the person guilty of wicked crimes against members of a particular family and this let their relatives to call the judiciary system **something**. For blank (i), the only possible alternatives can be '**set free**' or '**punish**'.

Fill-in 1 should be a word that relates to **set free** or **punish**.

Let us understand the meanings of the option words from blank (i).

(A) exculpate – show or declare that (someone) is not guilty of wrongdoing

(B) expurgate – remove matter thought to be objectionable or unsuitable from

(C) expatiate – speak or write in detail about

The correct answer for blank (i) is 'exculpate' since this matches the context of 'set free'. The word 'expurgate' though similar to 'punish' cannot work in a context of 'punishment' since 'expurgate' means to 'censor' or 'remove that which is offensive from a book or some form of medium'. The word 'expatiate' is not relevant to the context of the sentence.

Let us pre-empt **fill-in 2**. From context we know that the court set-free a man that was guilty of crimes. The next of kin must therefore have been very angry and even distraught about this decision. In context of 'this led the next of kin, who were present at the court hearing, to **say something** about the judiciary system' – we realize that they must have said something in a way to show anger or to demean. The word 'criticize' or 'scold' could work here.

Fill-in 2 should be a word that relates to **criticize** or **scold**.

Let us understand the meanings of the option words from blank (ii).

(D)   chastise – rebuke or reprimand severely

(E)   rhapsodize – speak or write about someone or something with great enthusiasm and delight

(F)   lubricate – make (a process) run smoothly

The correct answer for blank (ii) is 'chastise'. The word 'rhapsodize' is opposite of what the sentence requires. The word 'lubricate' is not relevant to the context o the sentence.

Let us pre-empt **fill-in 3**. From the context we realize that since the court did not apprehend the criminal and the next of kin were angry and 'chastised' the judiciary system. They must have called it a **'sham'** or **'joke'**.

Fill-in 3 should be a word that relates to **sham**.

Let us understand the meanings of the option words from blank (iii).

(G)   bastion – an institution, place, or person strongly maintaining particular principles, attitudes, or activities

(H)   travesty – a false, absurd, or distorted representation of something

(I)   laggard – a person who makes slow progress and falls behind others

The correct answer for blank (iii) is 'travesty'. Although 'laggard' brings a negative undertone there is nothing in the sentence that supports the context of 'slow progress' and the word 'laggard' is not as negative in tone as that of what is required by the sentence. The word 'bastion' is opposite of what the sentence requires.

The correct answers are A, D, & H.

96.   Let us understand the meanings of the sentences from the partial information.

The sentence discusses synaesthesia, which is commonly classified as a disability, yet occasionally it can be **something** to some people. For blank (i) the presence of the **signal word** **'yet'** and the **hint-phrase 'interpret the world in a completely novel way'** suggest that the supposed disability cold be a **benefit** for some people.

Fill-in 1 should be a word that relates to **benefit**.

Let us understand the meanings of the option words from blank (i).

(A)   advantageous – involving or creating favorable circumstances that increase the chances of success or effectiveness; beneficial

(B)   intense – of extreme force, degree, or strength

(C)   serious – significant or worrying because of possible danger or risk

The correct answer for blank (i) is 'advantageous' since this matches the context of 'benefit'. The word 'intense' and 'serious' are in contrast with what the sentence requires.

Let us pre-empt **fill-in 2**. Again as before the **hint-phrase 'interpret the world in a com-pletely novel way'** suggests that some people can use or **interpret** sensory impulses in a way that is completely different from normal.

Fill-in 2 should be a word that relates to **interpret**.

Let us understand the meanings of the option words from blank (ii).

(D)   cannot appreciate – cannot recognize the worth of

(E)   miss out on – fail to include someone or something; omit

(F)   can discern – can recognize

The correct answer for blank (ii) is 'can discern'. The other words are opposites of what the context requires.

Let us pre-empt **fill-in 3**. Since synaesthesia is advantageous for some and lets them discern sensory impulses in a way others can't. It probably inspires them into creating surreal works of art, which would have been **impossible to imagine** for a normal person.

Fill-in 3 should be a word that relates to **impossible to imagine**.

Let us understand the meanings of the option words from blank (iii).

(G)   inconceivable – not capable of being imagined or grasped mentally

(H)   indistinguishable – not able to be identified as different or distinct

(I)   appealing – interesting or attractive

The correct answer for blank (iii) is 'inconceivable'. The words 'indistinguishable' and 'appealing' do not fit the context of 'impossible to imagine'.

The correct answers are A, F, & G.

97.   Let us understand the meaning of the sentence from the partial information.

The sentence discusses Emily's recent novel. It says that the novel was criticized for its **some kind** of structure, since the writer was traditionally criticized for how her works generally are. For blank (ii), the **hint-word 'criticized'** suggests that her greatest **some-thing** about her works must refer to a negative quality. We need a word, which means **'weakness'**.

Fill-in 2 should be a word that relates to **weakness**.

Let us understand the meanings of the option words from blank (ii).

(D)   shortcoming – a fault or failure to meet a certain standard, typically in a person's character, a plan, or a system

(E)   preoccupation – the state or condition of being preoccupied or engrossed with some-thing

(F)   characteristic – typical of a particular person

The correct answer for blank (ii) is 'shortcoming'. The word 'preoccupation' does not relate to the context of the sentence. The word 'characteristic' does not bring in the negative undertone that the sentence requires.

Looking at the gist of the sentence, we realize that blank (i) and blank (ii) are related to each other. The presence of the **signal word 'ironically'** suggests that the relationship is contrasting in nature. Therefore **some kind** of structure her current work has and the **particular** kind of framework her works generally have must be contrasting in meaning. For blank (i), her latest work attracted criticism because of its either **adherence to** or **absence of** structure. Let's look at the options and pick ones that have opposing pairs.

Fill-in 1 should be a word that relates to either **adherence to** or **absence of**.

Let us understand the meanings of the option words from blank (i).

(A) attention to – giving lot of notice and care about

(B) parody of – mockery of

(C) lack of – absence of

For blank (i), the word 'parody of' doesn't fit the context of the sentence. The words 'attention to' and 'lack of' are both probable.

Let us understand the possible **fill-ins** for blank (iii).

We realize that if blank (i) is 'lack of' then blank (iii) must be a word which means '**extremely structured**'; if blank (i) is 'attention to', blank (iii) must be a word which means '**lacking structure**'.

Let us understand the meanings of the option words from blank (iii).

(G) relentlessly rigid – extremely rigid or non-flexible

(H) affably fatuous – lovably silly and unserious

(I) in comprehensively cryptic – extremely difficult to understand or figure-out

The correct answer for blank (iii) is 'relentlessly rigid' as this matches the context of 'extremely structured'. The other options do not match the context of either 'extremely structured' or 'lacking structure'.

Since blank (iii) is 'relentlessly rigid', blank (i) must be 'lack of'.

The correct answers are C, D, & G.

98. Let us understand the meaning of the sentence from the partial information.

The sentence discusses the drought of 1956 and the result it had. The sentence states that the drought resulted in a substantial **something** between crop supply and demand. Since this describes a drought, commonsense would dictate that production of crops would be drastically reduced, while demand will not necessarily reduce. Therefore, the word '**mismatch**' could work as **fill-in 1**.

Fill-in 1 should be a word that relates to **mismatch**.

Let us understand the meanings of the option words from blank (i).

(A) disparity – a great difference

(B) consanguinity – of people descended from the same ancestor

(C) heterogeneity – diversity in character or content

The correct answer for blank (i) is 'disparity' since this is line with the context of 'great mismatch in supply and demand'. The word 'heterogeneous' means 'different', but in context that the supply and demand was different doesn't bring to light the fact that there was a huge gap between the two – it only suggests that it was different. The word 'consanguinity' is not relevant to the context of the sentence.

For blank (ii); we notice that the sentence states that the prices became so **something**; the disparity in supply and demand as seen in this context would logically result in prices rocketing. The word '**inflated**' or '**excessive**' could work as **fill-in 2**.

Fill-in 2 should be a word that relates to either '**inflated**' or '**excessive**'.

Let us understand the meanings of the option words from blank (ii).

(D)   shielded – protected from changes or outside influence

(E)   depressed – in a lower position, having been pushed down

(F)   prohibitive – so high as to prevent something being done or bought

The correct answer for blank (ii) is 'prohibitive'. The words 'shielded' and 'depressed' create contexts that are opposites of what the sentence requires.

For blank (iii), in context the sentence suggests that prices were so 'prohibitive' that the suppliers were generally thought to be **doing something** to the customer. The word '**overcharging**' or '**cheating**' could work as **fill-in 3**.

Fill-in 3 should be a word that relates to **overcharging**.

Let us understand the meanings of the option words from blank (iii).

(G)   gouging – overcharging or swindling someone

(H)   blackmailing – demanding money from someone in return for not revealing compromising information which one has about them

(I)   placating – making less hostile

The correct answer for blank (iii) is 'gouging'; the word 'blackmailing' has no relevance in the context of this sentence. The word 'placating' is sort of opposite to what the sentence requires.

The correct answers are A, F, & G.

99.   Let us understand the meaning of the sentence from the partial information.

The sentence describes Rodrigues, stating that although Rodrigues could make himself look innovative; beneath the **something** he was actually rigid and uninspiring. For blank (iii), the **hint-phrase 'appear innovative and spontaneous'** suggests that beneath the '**appearance**' or '**act**', he remained uninspired and rigid.

Fill-in 3 should be a word that relates to **appearance** or **act**.

Let us understand the meanings of the option words from blank (iii).

(G)   guise – an external form, appearance, or manner of presentation, typically concealing the true nature of something

(H)   impeccability – of the highest standards; faultless

(I)   contriteness – expression of remorse at the recognition that one has done wrong

The correct answer for blank (iii) is 'guise'; the words 'impeccable' and 'contriteness' are not relevant to what the sentence requires.

For blank (ii); we notice that the sentence states that he **'appears'** to be innovative and spontaneous. This suggests that he was good at **pretending** to appear. **'Pretending'** can act as **fill-in 2**.

Fill-in 2 should be a word that relates to either **pretending**.

Let us understand the meanings of the option words from blank (ii).

(D) contriving – creating or bringing about (an object or a situation) through deliberate use of skill and artifice

(E) intending – planning or meaning to do or be the specified thing

(F) deserving – worthy of being treated in a particular way, typically of being given assistance

The correct answer for blank (ii) is 'contriving', since this brings in the aspect of 'creating something by being artificial or fake'. The words 'intending' and 'deserving' are not relevant to the context of the sentence.

For blank (i), through context we realize that he was **very skilled** at appearing in a particular way. **'Very skilled'** will act as **fill-in 1**.

Fill-in 1 should be a word that relates to **very skilled**.

Let us understand the meanings of the option words from blank (i).

(A) abstemious – indulging only very moderately in something, especially food and drink

(B) ingenious – clever, original, and inventive

(C) inept – having or showing no skill; clumsy

The correct answer for blank (i) is 'ingenious'; the word 'inept' is opposite of what the context requires. The word 'abstemious' is not relevant in context.

The correct answers are B, D, & G.

100. Let us understand the meaning of the sentence from the partial information.

The sentence describes Augustine and his philosophical theory. The only **hint-word** the sentence provides is the word **'infinite'**. Blank (i) states that he believes in a benevolent god of **something**. The something must have a positive undertone. Let's evaluate the options after understating their meanings.

Let us understand the meanings of the option words from blank (i).

(A) plentitude – abundance

(B) indulgence – the state or attitude of being indulgent or tolerant

(C) truculence – eagerness or quickness to argue or fight; aggressive defiance

The correct answer for blank (i) is 'plentitude'; the word 'truculence' is contrary to the connotation suggested by the sentence. The word 'indulgence', thought it seems relevant, actually has a negative undertone, and therefore doesn't fit the context of the sentence.

For blank (ii); similar to blank (i) we realize that we need a word with a positive undertone. Let us evaluate the answer options.

Let us understand the meanings of the option words from blank (ii).

(D) temperance – abstinence from alcoholic drink

(E) dissent – the offense of expressing disagreement with the referee's decision

(F) abundance – the state or condition of having a copious quantity of something; plentiful

The correct answer for blank (ii) is 'abundance'. The words 'temperance' and 'dissent' are not relevant to the context of the sentence.

For blank (iii), the context states that he **something** the concept of an infinite universe from the infinite god he believed in. Therefore he possibly **got inspiration for**.

Fill-in 3 should be a word that relates to **got inspiration for**.

Let us understand the meanings of the option words from blank (iii).

(G) arrogated – took or claimed (something) for oneself without justification

(H) separated – formed a distinction or boundary between

(I) derived – obtain something from (a specified source)

The correct answer for blank (iii) is 'derived' as the word matches the context of what the sentence requires. The word 'arrogated' brings a negative undertone that is not supported by the sentence. The word 'separated' does not match the context of the sentence.

The correct answers are A, F, & I.

Chapter 8

Answer key

8.1   Sentence Equivalence Questions

(1) A & E	(21) C & E	(41) A & C
(2) A & B	(22) B & C	(42) A & E
(3) A & F	(23) B & E	(43) A & E
(4) A & F	(24) A & C	(44) B & C
(5) A & E	(25) B & E	(45) C & D
(6) A & C	(26) B & E	(46) B & C
(7) B & C	(27) C & E	(47) B & E
(8) A & C	(28) A & D	(48) C & E
(9) A & D	(29) B & D	(49) B & F
(10) C & D	(30) A & D	(50) A & E
(11) C & F	(31) D & F	(51) A & C
(12) D & F	(32) A & E	(52) B & E
(13) C & F	(33) B & D	(53) D & E
(14) B & D	(34) A & C	(54) C & E
(15) C & E	(35) A & D	(55) A & D
(16) B & E	(36) A & B	(56) A & E
(17) A & C	(37) D & F	(57) A & D
(18) B & D	(38) D & F	(58) B & D
(19) A & D	(39) C & E	(59) B & E
(20) C & F	(40) A & D	(60) B & C

(61) C & E

(62) E & F

(63) C & F

(64) B & D

(65) D & F

(66) B & F

(67) C & F

(68) B & E

(69) C & D

(70) B & D

(71) A & D

(72) A & E

(73) B & F

(74) A & E

(75) A & F

(76) A & F

(77) A & E

(78) B & E

(79) A & E

(80) B & F

(81) D & F

(82) A & D

(83) C & D

(84) B & D

(85) B & E

(86) A & E

(87) B & C

(88) C & E

(89) A & D

(90) A & E

(91) A & E

(92) C & F

(93) A & B

(94) A & D

(95) A & E

(96) B & C

(97) C & D

(98) C & E

(99) E & F

(100) C & D

8.2   Text Completion Questions

(1) A	(28) A	(55) B & E
(2) C	(29) A	(56) C & D
(3) E	(30) E	(57) B & F
(4) A	(31) C	(58) A & E
(5) C	(32) C	(59) B & F
(6) B	(33) D	(60) B & D
(7) D	(34) B	(61) A & D
(8) D	(35) C	(62) C & E
(9) A	(36) A	(63) B & D
(10) D	(37) B	(64) A & D
(11) D	(38) E	(65) B & E
(12) A	(39) C	(66) B & D
(13) D	(40) D	(67) C & F
(14) D	(41) C	(68) B & D
(15) A	(42) C	(69) A & E
(16) A	(43) B	(70) A & E
(17) B	(44) C	(71) C & F
(18) C	(45) A	(72) C & E
(19) C	(46) C	(73) A & D
(20) D	(47) E	(74) B & E
(21) D	(48) E	(75) A & D
(22) A	(49) D	(76) A & D
(23) E	(50) C	(77) A & D
(24) B	(51) C & F	(78) B & D
(25) A	(52) B & E	(79) B & D
(26) D	(53) B & D	(80) B & F
(27) C	(54) B & F	(81) A, E & I
		(82) B, D & G
		(83) B, D & H

(84) A, E & G

(85) C, D & G

(86) C, E & G

(87) B, E & I

(88) C, E & H

(89) B, D & G

(90) C, D & G

(91) A, E & H

(92) B, F & I

(93) C, E & I

(94) B, F & G

(95) A, D & H

(96) A, F & G

(97) C, D & G

(98) A, F & G

(99) B, D & G

(100) A, F & I

Chapter 9

Talk to Us

Have a Question?

Please email your questions to info@manhattanreview.com. We will be happy to answer you. Your questions can be related to a concept, an application of a concept, an explanation of a question, a suggestion for an alternate approach, or anything else you wish to ask regarding the GRE.

Please do mention the page number when quoting from the book.

GRE - Resources from ETS

- *Official Guide*: It is one of the best resource to prepare for the GRE revised General test. It is a complete GRE book with everything you need to do your best on the test — and move toward your graduate or business school degree. It includes a couple of full-length practice test and two simulated, computer-based GRE practice tests., which help you measure your capability beforehand. The book also includes a *POWERPREP II* CD.

- *GRE Big Book*: It is a big fat book and includes 27 previously administered full-length tests. There are over 5000 actual ETS questions and answers. The strategies and tips to crack the computerized GRE is worth reading.

Manhattan Admissions

**You are a unique candidate with unique experience.
We help you to sell your story to the admissions committee.**

Manhattan Admissions is an educational consulting firm that guides academic candidates through the complex process of applying to the world's top educational programs. We work with applicants from around the world to ensure that they represent their personal advantages and strength well and get our clients admitted to the world's best business schools, graduate programs and colleges.

We will guide you through the whole admissions process:

- ☑ Personal Assessment and School Selection
- ☑ Definition of your Application Strategy
- ☑ Help in Structuring your Application Essays
- ☑ Unlimited Rounds of Improvement
- ☑ Letter of Recommendation Advice
- ☑ Interview Preparation and Mock Sessions
- ☑ Scholarship Consulting

To schedule a free 30-minute consulting and candidacy evaluation session or read more about our services, please visit or call:

 www.manhattanadmissions.com   +1.212.334.2500

Made in United States
North Haven, CT
05 June 2022

19870480R00113